Praise for *Partner Your Project*

"The County is committed to Partnering because the process works. We use Partnering on all our significant projects because it is good business — not because it is popular or trendy. We have seen that Partnering leads to timely resolution of problems or disputes, and results in more successful projects. It just makes sense. Read *Partner Your Project* and learn how to make partnering work for you."

Patrick Love
Senior Project Director
County of Santa Clara, California

"If you were to only read one book this year to improve your construction projects, *Partner Your Project* would be the one."

Joe Browne
Director, District 4
California Department of Transportation (Caltrans)

"Construction projects have become a war zone. Ms. Dyer's *Partner Your Project* is the manual for project peace."

Robert A. Rubin, Esq.
Partner and author of *Construction Claims Prevention and Resolution* and *New York Construction Law Manual*
Postner & Rubin

"*Partner Your Project* is a call to action for all of those who only give lip service to working together on construction projects. A highly interactive book, filled with exercises to help you understand the partnering process."

Dan Lowry
President
RGW Construction

"Filled with gems of practical wisdom from a true professional. Read it!"

Mike O'Brien
Program Manager
Turner Construction Company

"Every once in a while a book comes along that spells out the basics with simplicity and great insight. This is one of those books."

John E. Chiaverini
Assistant to the Chairman
Perini Corporation

"This book is written for those who want to improve their results. It will take you on a journey that can change your business…and your mind."

Chris Meyers
Director of Construction
ICF Kaiser Engineers, Inc.

"Sue Dyer's grace and enthusiasm for partnering comes across in each page of *Partner Your Project*. She shares with the reader her best ideas and years of experience."

Ray Rawcliffe, P.E., P.M.P
Program Manager
Pacific Gas and Electric Company

"Sue Dyer's *Partner Your Project* will help you create the synergy needed to inspire your team to unlock that elusive door to construction project success!"

Ed McCormick
Manager of Wastewater Design and Construction
East Bay Municipal Utility District
Oakland, California

Partner
YOUR
Project

Partner
YOUR
Project

SUE DYER

PENDULUM
PUBLISHING

Livermore, California 1997

First published August, 1997

10 9 8 7 6 5 4 3 2 1

Manufactured in the United States of America
ISBN 0-9652243-0-9

Library of Congress Cataloging-in-Publication Data

Dyer, Sue
    Partner Your Project : Working together to bring your
    project in on-time and on-budget... A step-by-step guide to
    partnering your project / Sue Dyer
        p.   cm.
    Includes bibliographical references
    ISBN 0-9652243-0-9
    1. Construction industry — ownership 2. Partnering 3.
    Business 4. Construction management I. Title
HD9715.A2.
624'.068—dc20   96-70849

The paper in this book meets the minimum requirements of the American National Standard for Information Services — Permanence of Paper for Printed Library Materials. ANSI Z39.49-1984

PENDULUM
PUBLISHING

Pendulum Publishing
1789 Barcelona Street
Livermore, California 94550

Dedication

1931-1995

Dedicated to the memory of DAN ANTOVICH
a true partnering pioneer

Acknowledgments

A book of this sort takes the effort of many dedicated people. It is with a great deal of pleasure and gratitude that I wish to thank them.

First, my husband Bruce Wiggs. Bruce acted as my chief editor and managed the entire publishing process. His attention to detail, support, and brilliant mind helped to mold the book into something truly worthwhile.

There were three professional editors who worked to get the words and sentences right: Dorris Lee, Bobbye Temple, and Claudia Stettler. Their loving touch helped to bring the text alive, but not kill the meaning.

I would like to thank all of my industry friends who became peer editors. Your comments were wonderful and offered many ideas which have been incorporated into the text. Thank you: Roger Brady, Mark Breslin, Joe Browne, Michel Caurant, Gary Cherrier, Jack Chevarini, John Costas, Dennis Dunne, Pete Fusselman, Steve Geney, George Gipe, Ron Klimczak, Pat Love, Jim Martin, Marlene Martin, Kathy Mayo, Ed McCormick, Chris Meyer, Jerry Overaa, Lora Peluso, Larry Rasumssen, Ray Rawcliffe, Jim Siebe, Michael Strogoff, Gary Veerkamp, and Joe Woods.

Many industry leaders were willing to offer praise for *Partner Your Project*, and I thank you; Mark Breslin, Joe Browne, John Chiaverini, Peter Fusselman, Pat Love, Dan Lowry, Ed McCormick, Chris Meyer, Henry Michel, Mike O'Brien, Ray Rawcliffe, Linda Rhodes, Bob Rubin.

I would like to thank Russ Chaney and Lora Peluso for helping to formulate the idea for the book, Tom Okarma for writing a foreword, and DPIC for its support of the book and partnering.

George Foster designed a great cover and helped to assure the book jacket was printed as designed. Thanks, George.

Diane and Chuck Jeronimo helped to proofread the final edited version.

Many worked to bring you this book. I hope you enjoy it, and use it to help bring your projects in on-time and on-budget.

Foreword

Dear Reader,

DPIC believes in partnering — believes so strongly that it offers to fund partnering workshops on the projects it insures. We foster the use of partnering on construction projects because of its power to prevent or significantly reduce the impact of disputes.

Sue Dyer's new book, *Partner Your Project*, explains this approach to loss prevention. This innovative book is practical, user friendly, and will help both beginners and experienced partnering veterans understand the partnering process, and how to avoid its pitfalls.

We at DPIC would like to express our thanks to Sue Dyer, one of the pioneers of the partnering movement, for sharing her unique insights and innovative approaches in *Partner Your Project*.

Thomas M. Okarmo, CPCU
President and Chief Executive Officer
Design Professional Insurance Companies, Inc.

How to Use this Book

Project partnering is a dynamic process which is always changing with the situation, people and issues. This book has been designed to help you learn to optimize the partnering process on your projects. Successful project partnering is part art and part skill. *Partner Your Project* takes you through the entire process of partnering; from deciding to partner, selecting a project, getting everyone onboard, the steps to successfully partner, and explains how partnering is being used in ever expanding ways.

Depending on your need, you may select to start at a particular section of the book. Whether you are curious about partnering, wanting to learn more about how to assure partnering success, or trying to convince your project team to partner your project, I hope you will let *Partner Your Project* be your guide.

Ways For You To Use This Book

■ **As a gift to help** convince potential project partners of the value of partnering.

■ **As a how-to manual** for those new to partnering who want to assure its success.

■ **As an overview and guide** for partnering veterans who want to continue to improve their partnering results.

■ **As a reference book** for project managers (and others) from all stakeholder groups, who are in the trenches day-to-day and need a reference to help them stay on track with their partnering effort and help assure the success of their project.

Deciding Where to Start

Part 1 The Benefits of Partnering Your Project
Part one answers the question often asked, "Why should I partner my project"? Knowing the benefits of partnering can help you understand why you should partner your projects. This can also be shared with potential project team mem-

bers who might be reluctant to partner. This broad overview of the benefits can be revisited time and again to remind everyone what it is you are seeking, together.

Part 2 *A Brief Overview of Partnering*

This partnering overview explains how partnering came about in the design and construction industry, and offers an understanding of the partnering process and theories on what it takes to make it successful for your project.

Part 3 *Five Steps To Partnering Your Project*

The five steps to partnering your project takes you through the nuts and bolts of how to successfully partner your project. This part contains a process which, if followed, can help assure your partnering success.

Part 4 *Special Applications of Partnering*

Partnering is expanding into new applications all the time. Partnering is also the first line of defense against litigation in an expanding arena of alternative dispute resolution processes. Part IV will walk you through some new applications of the partnering process and what is happening in ADR in our industry.

Contents

Figures

0

A Partnering Parable

> *...everything can be taken from a man but one thing: the last of the human freedoms — to choose one's attitudes in any given set of circumstances, to choose one's own way.*
>
> Viktor E. Frankl, *Man's Search for Meaning*

There is an old tale which goes:

And the Lord said to the Rabbi, *"Come, I will show you hell."*

They entered a room where a group of people sat around a huge pot of stew. Everyone was famished and desperate. Each held a spoon that reached the pot but had a handle so long that it could not be used to reach their mouths. The suffering was terrible.

"Come, now I'll show you Heaven," the Lord said after a while.

They entered another room, identical to the first — the pot of stew, the group of people, the same long spoons. But, there, everyone was happy and nourished.

"I don't understand," said the Rabbi. *"Why are they happy here when they were miserable in the other room, and everything is the same?"*

The Lord smiled. *"Ah, but don't you see?"* the Lord asked. *"Here they have learned to feed each other."*

It is not our circumstances but our ability and willingness to work together that makes the difference between heaven and hell

It is not our circumstances but our ability and willingness to work together that makes the difference between heaven and hell. Even in the toughest circumstances people who pull together can find creative solutions to their problems.

When we resist working together and look for someone or something to blame for our problems, fear takes over and the stage is set for battle. Settlement often comes only when an authority pronounces who wins and who loses. The problems often remain unsolved with the relationship in ruins. No progress has been made and much has been lost, in emotions, energy, and future opportunities. Rest assured that those who lost will not soon forget, and even if you were declared the victor in this battle, the loser will wait for his next chance to battle with you.

Even in the toughest circumstances, people who pull together can find creative solutions to their problems

Over the past twenty-plus years construction projects have become adversarial. Too often the project team members fear their individual potential liability and become protective. As a result, communication breaks down or stops, trust erodes, and, over time, everyone on the project shifts into a survival mode. Starving, suffering, everyone is looking for a way out alive.

Owners, contractors, architects, engineers, and construction managers all recognize the problem and have been seeking new project delivery systems and new ways of contracting — but find ultimately that they are seeking a way to fairly manage the risk to everyone involved. Partnering seems to be the best answer so far.

Partnering is a process which allows people working together to find and build on their common ground

Partnering is a process which allows people working together to find and build on their common ground and co-create solutions to problems, seeking mutual benefit. By building a good working relationship, the partnering process can help create an atmosphere where trust and communication can flourish.

This book will take you through the process for deciding, selling, developing, and implementing a successful partnering process on your project(s).

PART 1

The Benefits of Partnering Your Project

1
Stay Out of Court

Discourage litigation. Persuade your neighbors to compromise when-ever you can. Point out how the nominal winner is often the real loser — in fees, expenses, and waste of time.

Abraham Lincoln

Almost everyone who has been in design and construction, or business in general for that matter, has been involved in litigation. You know how valuable a good attorney can be to you and your organization. Our system of law, the underpinning of our form of government, depends on the legal profession for its implementation. In the last few decades the legal industry has moved away from being the upholders of law and pursuers of justice into being a "sue for profit" industry.

The costs for litigation run as high as $60 billion a year

An Explosion of Litigation

Almost no one approaches a project today without keeping in mind that they might be sued, or how they might sue someone else. Far too often a project is looked at as a potential liability instead of as a challenge to be taken. This thinking costs everyone time and money, and results in added stress. Today, many in the industry feel that design and construction just aren't fun anymore.

Far too often a project is looked at as a potential liability instead of as a challenge

Sue-For-Profit Industry

A New York businessman told the Wall Street Journal, "It's just a jumble of litigation… all you need is a good lawyer and you can tie up somebody's bid for a year." Protesting bids, creating claims, pushing risk on anyone available, and refusing to accept responsibility have become a natural part of doing business. And, if in the end, you fail to make a profit, or the project costs more than you want, you will have created enough documentation for a rip-roaring lawsuit to try and recapture your losses or cost overruns.

Over the past decade there has been an explosion of construction-related litigation. Some say the tab runs as high as $60 billion a year. A Texas professor, Steven Maggee, conducted research to discover the impact of having a growing number of lawyers in the United States. Although controversial, his findings are interesting. According to Maggee, for each lawyer in the country, and each new lawyer who passes the bar, the gross domestic product loses a million dollars each year[1]. The loss occurs in higher prices charged due to potential liability, and in products and services that never get to market because they are deemed too risky.

As the volume of legal actions has increased, decisions have become more erratic and inconsistent, leaving everyone wondering what the law really means

Litigation Paradigm Shift

As the pots of money won from lawsuits have grown, more people have looked to "make their killing" in the courts. The promise was that the more lawyering went on, the better and fairer life in America would be. The signs are otherwise. As the volume and intensity of their output has risen, our courts, rather than converging with new confidence on important truths, have become more random and inconsistent in their pronouncements.[2] This is not a comforting thought when you feel you have been wronged.

The current sue-for-profit industry was born out of the belief that private quarrels should lead to public benefit

Lawsuits (it now began to be urged) should be seen not just as ways to clarify the bounds between two private rights that might have come into conflict, but as campaigns to liberate people whose rights had been insolently trod on. In fact, even more important than to liberate existing victims was to deter future treadings-on of rights.[3]

Before long, lawsuits were being praised to the skies as highly productive and public-spirited enterprises. To file a one, it was argued, was to do a commendable service to the general populace, far over and above any incidental benefit to oneself. The bold new twist was the idea that private quarrels also lead to public benefit; the more fights you get into, the better a place you make the world for everyone else.[4] Thus was born the current sue-for-profit industry.

Lawyers - Unparalleled Power

In *The Litigation Explosion*, Walter K. Olson states: "America is the litigious society it is because American lawyers wield such unparalleled powers of imposition. No other country gives a private lawyer such a free hand to select a victim, tie him up in court on undefined charges, force him to hire lawyers of his own at dire expense, trash his privacy through we-have-ways-of-making-you-talk discovery, wear him down on the perpetual-motions treadmill, libel him grossly in documents that become permanent public records, and keep him scrambling to respond to Gryo Gearloose experts and Game of the States conflicts theories."[5]

The primary concern of designers, contractors, and construction lawyers surveyed was that the involvement of lawyers actually tends to slow up the resolution process

Lawyers have the power to control the destiny of almost any type of dispute. Many feel that truth, fairness and equity are not any longer a part of the judicial process. Given the billions of dollars per year the "lawsuit" industry yields, lawyers have not just sat back and watched the money roll in. They have shrewdly invested their wealth and power in the currency of political and ideological influence.[6] The trial lawyers organization has become one of the most powerful lobby groups in America.

In a survey of designers, contractors, and construction lawyers conducted by the University of Washington, more than one-third of the respondents said that their primary concern when obtaining the services of a lawyer is that the resolution of the issue is not timely and that the involvement of the lawyers actually tends to slow up the resolution process. Several stated that the presence of a lawyer hinders open communication between disputing parties and, in fact, contributes to polarizing their positions. [7]

Believing that there must be a better way, partnering began to explode on the scene in the late 1980s

Partnering: A Way Out

Frustrated with the time, cost, energy and ineffectiveness of settling construction disputes in the courts, many in the industry believed there must be a better way. Partnering began to explode on the scene in the late 1980s.

Partnering offers a means by which all the project stakeholders come together to get to know each other and agree on a way of approaching a project. Trust and fairness are key values of the partnership. Also developed is an agreed-upon process for resolving disputes should they arise. This approach has been so effective that, at a conference I attended in Kentucky, one construction lawyer stood up and said that if partnering and other forms of alternative dispute resolution continue to be as effective as they have been over the past few years, the construction lawyer will be history in another five years. Now, no one believes that there won't be any construction lawyers, however, they are working to redefine their roles in helping their clients. Partnering is proving to be successful for all concerned.

Partnering results have been so consistent and dramatic, that the insurance industry is beginning to recognize that partnering substantially limits the risk of litigation and disputes

Partnering results have been so consistent and dramatic, that the insurance industry is beginning to recognize that partnering substantially limits the risk of litigation and disputes, and has developed programs which pay for the partnering facilitator. One example is the Design Professional Insurance Companies which offer a program called

2

Don't Let the Past Predict Your Project's Future

The past does not equal the future.

Anthony Robbins

Overcoming Our Adversarial Mind-set

Chapter 1 described how the explosion of litigation has complicated the construction industry and made it difficult and unfulfilling to work on many projects. But there has been an even more fundamental shift as a result of this explosion of litigation. The industry has accepted the judicial system's paradigm as its own business paradigm.

The judicial system was designed to be adversarial

Adversarial by Design

The judicial system was designed to be adversarial; each side taking a position and arguing that position in front of an impartial jury or judge. The outcome is that someone wins and someone loses.[9] This is a classic example of a zero-sum game. In order for someone to win a dollar, someone else must lose a dollar. This win/lose approach to the business of design and construction has eroded the industry's ability to create new solutions to today's problems. Those using this approach look for blame, not for solutions. They seek to win, and to make the other guy lose.

The win/lose approach to the business of design and construction has eroded the industry's ability to create new solutions to today's problems

A construction project brings together many people, each offering special expertise, ability and interests. What one does impacts the next, and so on. Because so many interests overlap, the adversarial approach causes good business decision-making to break down, and everyone ends up losing. Control of the decision-making is taken out of the hands of the people involved and given to someone else.

To make things different, everyone must change. Partnering offers a new paradigm for working together: cooperation and solving problems for mutual gain. Creativity is allowed to develop to help people find ways to solve problems that are good for everyone concerned. Or, to find ways to manage conflicting interests in an agreed-upon manner that everyone feels is fair.

Partnering offers a new paradigm for working together — cooperation

You Get What You Expect

Many years ago, a study was conducted in a San Francisco school. On the first day of class two teachers were called separately into the principal's office. The first was congratulated and told that she had been selected to have a class filled with gifted students — the brightest of the bright students — and that he knew she would have a great year. Additionally, she was warned that at no time was she allowed to tell anyone what she had been told. The second teacher also was congratulated, but was told that because he had such a great way with children that he would rise to the challenge of having a class filled with the lowest scoring children in the district's history. He also was not to tell anyone.

The Pygmalion effect states that you get what you expect from people — be it good or bad

The reality was that each of these teachers' classes was comprised of a normal mixture of bright, average and slower children, just as was every other class in the school.

At the end of the year the results were astounding. The teacher with the "gifted" class had the highest scores ever achieved on the district's achievement test. The teacher with the "lowest scoring" class did, in fact, score the lowest scores ever in the district's history.

This experiment has been repeated hundreds of times with the same result, called the Pygmalion effect. You get what you expect, no matter what the ability of others involved.

The people on your project are no different. To get different results, you have to change your expectations.

Partnering gives you an opportunity to examine your expectations and create new ones: expectations of working together to design and build the best project possible.

Don't Let History Repeat Itself

If at any time you are not getting the results you desire, you'd better check to see what underlying expectations might be at work.

We all have what we think are logical reasons for believing what we do about "him" or "her." That person has a reputation or a history with us that makes us expect the worst. Our mind, especially our subconscious, has a way of taking what has happened in the past and projecting it into the present and on out into the future. We can be fairly accurate at predicting the future because we have already determined that it will be like the past.

In partnering sessions the participants usually do an exercise to better understand the beliefs and stereotypes that we have about each other. This is often illuminating, and almost always negative. These negative expectations color the relationships on the project. Without doing something to overcome these negative expectations, and replacing them with ones you want to have on your project, you are destined to repeat history, over and over and over.

Partnering gives you control over what kind of working relationship you want. It allows you to determine how you want to communicate, cooperate, and deal with conflict and any other challenge you foresee. You are not a pebble in the stream getting pushed along by the current; you can take charge and work to create the project you want.

No Contract Can Be Written That Can Replace Trust

You could hire the best team of lawyers and experts and still you would not be able to write a contract that can re-

Partnering gives you an opportunity to examine your expectations about others and create new ones

Partnering gives you control over what kind of working relationship you want

place trust. After all, a contract is a promise to do something. Trust is its foundation. When trust erodes on a project, communication stops and positioning letters start to fly. Everyone begins to look for a scapegoat or someone they can blame.

Norm Anderson, a fellow partnering facilitator with Resolutions International, shared with me the following story. On a jobsite where thousands of yards of concrete were being poured, an inspector's truck stood nearby. As you approached the truck you could see there were small figures neatly painted on the fender. These figures were of concrete trucks. Just as a fighter pilot would track his kills on the side of his plane, or a football player would track his hits on the side of his helmet, this inspector placed one concrete truck on the side of his pickup for each load of concrete he rejected.

A contract is just a promise to do something — trust is its foundation

This story reflects the attitudes many owners, contractors and designers have toward one another. Lack of trust and a belief that you are supposed to be enemies, at battle, keeps many projects from being successful. Attitudes such as being the concrete police, as this inspector saw his role, keeps everyone from doing what is best for the project, stuck in fighting for their interests rather than working together collaboratively to solve the problem.

The erosion of trust has created a blizzard of paperwork

The erosion of trust has created a blizzard of paperwork. Documentation. Documentation. Documentation. CYA. There were three identical projects along a freeway system. One project was partnered and there were no pending claims. The project to the south had not been partnered. There were 1,200 letters of potential claims pending at the end of the project. The project team decided that they were certainly going to partner the project in the middle. That middle project ended up being far more difficult than either of the other two as substantial hazardous materials were found on the site and the job was shut down for four months. But, two years into the project, there are no pending claims. Partnering really helps!

3

A More Effective Way for Working Together

Q. You quoted penal experts as saying three out of four murderers have less than average intelligence. Do they mean murder itself is stupid?
A. Pretty close. University studies suggest murder usually occurs because the murderer doesn't have enough imagination to solve the problem any other way.

San Francisco Chronicle Answer Man

A New Paradigm for a New Age

Runaway litigation isn't the only force changing the design and construction industry. Increasing competition has decreased the bid price for most types of projects, but has not decreased costs. Profit margins continue to shrink as the price of labor and materials continues to increase, and as we continue to face foreign competition. Increasing regulation and environmental pressures add to the cost and complexity of every project. The banking crisis has tightened the supply of money for funding private projects and for working capital. Public works funding also has been affected, as politicians face a growing sentiment that government is too big and inefficient to decide what needs to be done. Government agencies are being pushed into re-engineering themselves from "stagnant bureaucracies" into downsized, flexible, service-minded organizations. Services previously performed by government employees are being contracted out as budgets are cut. The remaining employees are often fearful and bitter. Given these feelings, in addition to an increased workload, circumstances are ripe for conflict and

There is little doubt that the industry is entering a new age and those in the industry must change

disputes. There is little doubt that the industry is entering a new age — the information age of the twenty-first century — and those in the industry must change.

To be successful in this new age, a new paradigm for working together harmoniously must be found. Partnering is this paradigm. A definition of partnering is: two or more individuals, organizations, or communities, working together cooperatively, despite their differences, toward a mutually beneficial outcome.

Partnering: two or more individuals, organizations, or communities, working together cooperatively, despite their differences, toward a mutually beneficial outcome

The partnering approach offers a new way of looking at projects and relationships. Partnering is a non-adversarial approach to dealing with people. Instead of looking at someone as your "opponent" you look at them as your "partner." The goal of partnering is to create solutions, not winners and losers. By focusing on solutions you will be able to find creative ways to allow everyone to have what they need. The adversarial approach is based on fear, which results in a defensive posture. Partnering is based on trust, which results in an offensive posture. Partnering is focused on self-control, as opposed to abdicating responsibility to a third party, such as a judge or jury. Conflict is made to be productive rather than destructive. The result for all project stakeholders is positive change rather than nonproductive rigidity.

Partnering also works to maximize opportunities. When fear is driven out of relationships and replaced by trust, creativity abounds. New insights build and an atmosphere of innovation results. Cooperation leads to collaboration, which leads to innovation. Total quality management and continuous improvement thrive in such an atmosphere.

Cooperation leads to collaboration, which leads to innovation

Find and Build on Common Ground

Thirty years ago it was common for owners (even public owners) to meet with the designer and contractor over lunch to talk about a project, cut deals and make agreements. Today, in our highly litigious and regulated atmosphere, most public officials would not dare to even appear that they let a contractor or designer buy them lunch. Partnering offers a means by which that same kind of conversation from the past can take place today.

Frequently, at the beginning of a partnering workshop, each group is apprehensive about the others. They are afraid they will somehow be given less than what they deserve, so they are cautious. As we move through the day, and each group shares what their interests are, that is, what they want to get from the project, each group begins to see that there are many common interests. In fact, most of the interests are the same. Everyone wants the project to be on time (time is money), within budget (everyone's budget), be of high quality (no re-work, and easy maintenance), be safe (no one wants anyone to be hurt), and so on.

Getting to Know Each Other As People

One of the most profound results of attending a partnering workshop is that you get to know the other project team members as people. Each has strengths, weaknesses, likes, dislikes, and a life away from the project. They are people. Some you will like and become friends with; others you may want to keep at a professional distance. But you will still know each other. When you call on the phone, you will know who that person is. She has two children, went to the same university as your brother and loves skiing. It's much harder to write a positioning letter to someone you know.

Even if by some chance you find out at your partnering session that you don't like most of the people on your project team, that in itself is important information to have. Now you know what approach you might want to use in dealing with them. You don't have to like each other to be an effective project team. You just have to be willing to be fair with each other.

Working Together, not Against Each Other

It is difficult to design or build a project without cooperation. Far too often I see people working against each other, all the while trying to bring the project in on time and within budget. This is next to impossible. If you and I were setting out to climb to the top of a mountain, and we were not go-

One of the most profound results of attending a partnering workshop is that you get to know the other project team members as people

You don't have to like each other to be an effective project team — you just have to be willing to be fair with each other

19

ing to cooperate on the way up, but rather work against each other all the way, how efficient would we be in time and energy spent? If we set out on the same trek and cooperated on the way up, how much faster do you think we would make it to the top? Ten times faster? One hundred times faster? Working together you can gather the best information available, and make the best decisions possible, in the least amount of time, helping each other along the way.

4

Manage Project Risks

Why do I subscribe to partnering? Because it works! It works because neither party can afford failure.

Joe Browne, Director,
California Department of Transportation,
District #4

Risks

Projects are fraught with risk. Dealing effectively and fairly with risk exponentially increases your chances for success. At a meeting I attended, a man stood up and said that a study showed that over 90 percent of disputes ending in litigation were relationship-based, not technically-based. If we are to believe this man's statement, then it is obvious that the best way to decrease your risk is to improve your relationships. Here are six common relationship risks. These risks threaten the project and the team's ability to bring the project in on time and on budget. The partnering process and spirit naturally manages these risks.

Risk of Poor Communication

Open, honest and good lines of communication are paramount for your project's success. Purposefully keeping quiet so as not to let people know your interests, writing letters to communicate instead of talking to each other, and blaming others for the problems on the project all lead to poor communication.

Partnering helps to create an atmosphere where open, honest and frank conversation can occur without judgment or reprisal.

Over 90 percent of disputes ending in litigation were relationship-based, not technically-based

Risk of Poor Coordination

It is a law of physics that two objects cannot occupy the same space at the same time. Yet many times that is what projects try to do. Often, after much tension and confusion as to who is to do what, and when, it is discovered that there was a fundamental misunderstanding of the roles and responsibilities of the various team members.

Often, after much confusion, it is discovered that there was a fundamental misunderstanding of the roles and responsibilities of the various team members

Partnering gives everyone an opportunity to discover each other's role in the project, their scope and schedule, what they hope to gain, and their level of authority, so better coordination is possible.

Risk of Poor Decision-Making

Research has shown that once decisions leave the project level, costs increase.[10] Poor decisions are made when the best information is not available and when priorities cannot be set. Without seeing the whole picture, it is difficult at best to decide on a direction. This can result in lost time, extreme caution, fragmented decisions, lack of action, and the placing of blame. When each problem is equally as important as the next, and the next and then the next, it becomes exceedingly difficult to make a decision on what to do.

Partnering teaches a process for problem-solving and decision-making which can be translated to the field. But more than that, it develops an atmosphere where information flows freely so good decisions can be made in a timely fashion. Also, your partnering mission and goals help to set your priorities — you know where you are aiming.

Once decisions leave the project level, costs increase

Risk of Time Delays

Unforeseen conditions, lack of cooperation and coordination, changes in design, and a myriad of other factors threaten the schedule. Time has become such a large hammer that contractors are often extremely fearful of giving the owner and architect an accurate schedule from which they could effectively manage the project. As a backlash, many projects end up with multiple schedules: the one that meets the contract requirements; the one that you really expect to meet; and the one you hope to meet. Not only does this fear lead to untold risk, it also makes it difficult to deal effectively with changes.

Fairness and cooperation are the cornerstones to partnering. In many partnering sessions the team members agree on the function of the schedule and determine if they will use multiple schedules as tools for managing the project. This is done in the open, so everyone has the same information.

Risk of Losing Money

Protecting project costs, whether you are the owner or contractor, is a common goal. As costs escalate, someone has to pay them. This can cause enormous conflict and tension between project members.

Time has become such a large hammer that contractors are often extremely fearful of giving the owner and architect an accurate schedule

Partnering helps to develop a relationship where open discussion and understanding can be achieved, so that a determination of what is fair for all involved can be achieved. This is often not easy, but best done as soon as possible. You will never have fresher information and a better understanding of the situation, even if it is impossible to determine the ultimate impacts. Partnering allows dialogue to start and continue, and for fair agreements to be struck.

Personal Risks

In some firms, both public and private, you are seen to be only as good as your last project. Career advancement and rewards are often on the line with each new project.

Fairness and cooperation are the cornerstones of partnering

Partnering helps foster relationships between people. This includes those people in your own organization with whom you wish to be seen and to be known. Being able to effectively foster the partnering concept can lead to your advancement.

5

Improve Productivity, Quality and Job Satisfaction

*The failure of Total Quality Management programs has many reasons, but fundamentally you can't have continuous improvement without a foundation of **trust**. It's like having your foot on the gas and brake at the same time.*

Peter Drucker

Looking for Improved Productivity

In the early 1980s, the Business Round Table, a group of chief executive officers from over 200 major companies, was looking for ways to improve productivity in the construction industry. At the time construction was the only major industry that had consistently lower productivity each year for fifteen years.[10] Construction is perhaps the only industry which impacts every other industry. Every business and organization must have a building in which to operate, roads and bridges on which to ship its goods and for its people to travel to work on, and homes for its employees. So every nonproductive construction dollar indirectly impacts the gross domestic product.

> *The construction industry was the only major industry that had consistently lower productivity each year for fifteen years*

With this in mind, an *outrageous* program, called Tripartite, was tried. This was the first attempt on a project to bring together the owner, contractors and labor. The goal was to foster cooperation and communication. Even though most people at the time thought the idea was completely insane, the projects that tried this "insane" idea showed significant improvements.

Today, the idea of project stakeholders coming together to partner has become accepted. And while the Tripartite (partnering) effort has had success in achieving its initial goal of stopping runaway litigation, it is also achieving an unexpected benefit: improved project productivity.

The idea of project stakeholders coming together to partner has become accepted

The Construction Industry Institute (CII) conducted a bench-mark study. It concluded that partnering, properly imple-mented, can produce significant benefits. One of the key findings was that all companies (owners and contractors) practicing partnering are experiencing savings in total in-stalled project costs. As you can see below, saving ranged between four and twenty-five percent for the owner and between seven and thirty percent for contractors.

One of the key findings was that all companies (owners and contractors) practicing partnering are experiencing savings in total installed project costs

Expected Savings: Total Installed Costs

	Owner	Contractor	Total
High	25%	30%	30%
Median	13%	10%	10%
Low	4%	7%	4%

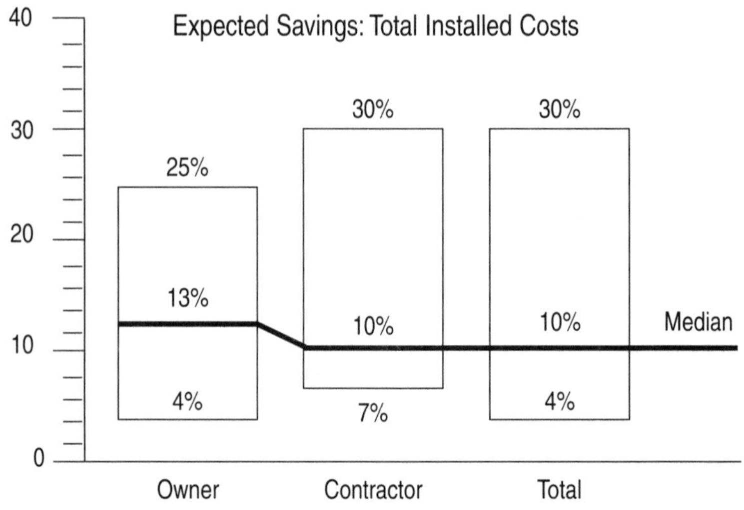

Source: CII News - September 1994

Figure 1

Clearly, partnering offers not only reduced liability, but an opportunity for increased productivity and profit for all parties.

Quality Results

Total quality management has never been fully embraced by the design and construction industry. Each job changes every day, and the techniques developed for manufacturing simply don't work. The quality manager of a large utility company stood up in one of my partnering sessions and announced that partnering was the best process he had ever seen for quality improvement. As the quote at the beginning of this chapter states, it is impossible to have continuous improvement without trust. Partnering helps develop the atmosphere of trust that makes quality possible.

The Quality Manager of a large utility company stood up in one of my partnering sessions and announced that partnering was the best process he had ever seen for quality improvement

> **Partnering is an excellent vehicle for attaining TQM in the construction process. An effective partnering relationship will facilitate improved quality by replacing the adversarial atmosphere of traditional business relationships with a team approach to achieve common goals. Team members can challenge directives when the impact on the work affects quality or is disproportionate to the benefits. The potential for improved quality also is increased to a better understanding of project scope and an atmosphere more conducive to implementing new technologies.**
>
> "In Search of Partnering Excellence"
> Construction Industry Institute
> Special Publication 17-1, July 1991

Numerous other studies and reports have been developed by the likes of:

Arizona Department of Transportation
Washington State Department of Transportation
U.S. Army Corps of Engineers
Federal Highway Administration
Dispute Avoidance and Resolution Task Force (DART)
Design Professionals Insurance Company
American Bar Association
Texas Department of Transportation

It is impossible to have continuous improvement without trust

Each indicates that partnering is improving construction quality. Partnering offers a vehicle for owners to save money and for contractors to improve their bottom line.

Improved Job Satisfaction

Dreading to get up and go to work literally kills people. Stress and frustration lead to many kinds of physical and psychological ailments. Getting back to enjoying the challenge of design and construction and working together to complete the project, go a long way toward increasing job satisfaction. Partnering is no panacea, but it offers a tool for working out problems and opening up communication, and, as a result, makes the job more enjoyable.

Partnering offers a tool for working out problems, opening up communication, solving problems, and, as a result, makes the job more enjoyable

I once heard a contractor tell his people that he paid them to work, not to be happy. Obviously he was not aware that happier people tend to be more productive. We don't need a county club atmosphere, but rather the feeling that you can say what's on your mind without being punished. And, equally important, that you have some control over your day-to-day work. Without that, frustration mounts and at some point the volcano blows. Partnering improves job satisfaction.

Partnering: A Cooperative Advantage

If partnering reduces the total installed costs for projects, then what might be its long-term effect on the construction and building industry?

First, partnering becomes the price of entrance into the marketplace. Contractors who develop a partnering culture within their organizations will, as a result, be more competitive. If the average profit for a contractor is 3 percent, and if by partnering he can increase his bottom line by 2-3 percent, then it is possible for him to be more competitive and more profitable.

Partnering will become the cost of entry into the construction market

This evolution is shown in the figure on the facing page. The process starts by indicating that both the owner and contractor have reduced installed costs by 2-3 percent. The contractor's profit is now 5 percent and we can assume the owner saved 5 percent (see graph on page 29). The contractor's increased profit will appear attractive to other contractors who want to have a piece of the pie. So other contractors using partnering will bid jobs based on the lower costs that partnering brings. This results in lowering bid prices. Contractors unable or unwilling to use partnering will find themselves becoming uncompetitive. Eventually, contractors' profits will return to an equilibrium. No one knows what that is, but let's assume it is 3 percent.

It will take time for contractors to learn to partner well. Those who partner well now have a definite competitive advantage

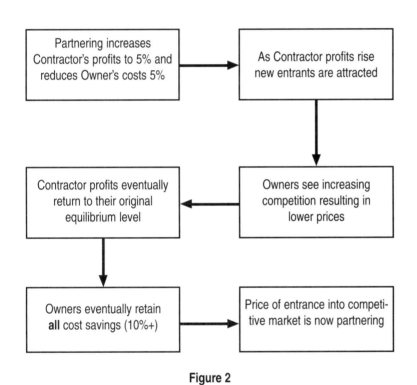

Figure 2

As a result, over the long-term, all cost savings will be retained by the owner, and the price of entrance into this competitive market will be your ability to partner well. It will take time for contractors to learn to partner well. Those who partner well now have a definite competitive advantage, and will continue to have it until others catch up.

PART 2

A Brief Overview of Partnering

6

The History of Partnering

In the last chapter we talked about how in the early 1980s the Business Round Table was looking for ways to improve productivity in the construction industry. The story continues in this chapter.

Private Partnering Takes Hold

Total quality management spread through most industries during the latter half of the 1980s. The United States was scrambling to find ways to become competitive in our own country. The Japanese and other foreign countries were making quality products and Americans were buying them. Dr. W. Edwards Deming, generally regarded as the leader in quality management, was instrumental in helping the postwar Japanese become world quality leaders. Over the course of his work, Dr. Deming developed his fourteen Points which are elaborated at length in his capstone work, *Out of Crisis*.[11] Three of Dr. Deming's celebrated fourteen Points particularly influenced the birth of the partnering concept in the private sector.

> In the 1980s the United States was scrambling to find ways to become competitive in our own country

■ **Adopt a new philosophy**. We are in a new economic age. Western management must awaken to the challenge, must learn their responsibilities, and take on leadership for change.

■ **End the practice of awarding business on the basis of price alone**. Instead, minimize total cost. Move toward a single supplier for any one item, on a long-term relationship of loyalty and trust.

■ **Drive out fear**, so that everyone may work effectively for the company.

These concepts led to the development of strategic alliances among owners and suppliers, including their designers and contractors. Thus, striving for improved quality and competitive advantage, partnering was born in the private sector. In these private partnerships it was felt that in order to

Partnering was born in the private sector, where it was thought that in order to partner you must have a long-term relationship

For some time it was believed that public sector construction partnering was impractical, if not impossible

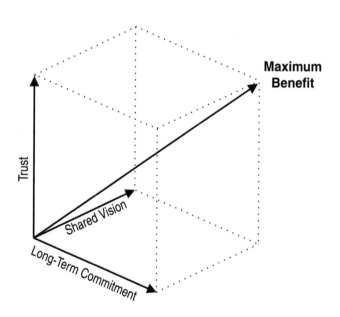

Source: In Search of Partnering Excellence, CII Special Publication 17-1, July 1991

Figure 3

"partner" you must have a long-term relationship. For some time, it was believed that public sector construction partnering was impractical, if not impossible. A few pioneers persisted.

Public Partnering Is Born

In 1987 Colonel Charles Cowan of the U. S. Army Corps of Engineers in Oregon and Norm Anderson[*] of the Washington State Department of Transportation, simultaneously began to develop cooperative programs for their public projects. These programs began to be called "public partnering." Within a couple of years 85 percent of the state departments of transportation were partnering.[12] Partnering spread like wildfire to many public owners who developed partnering specifications, and began to define what partnering meant to their organization.

In the public sector, the award of contracts to the lowest responsible bidder is customary. Trying to develop a partnership with someone who was the low bidder on a project seemed difficult at best, and downright unattractive to some owners. But as public owners and contractors heard of partnering successes, they gave it a try. Some met with tremendous success, and others with very little. But over time public partnering is becoming a standard tool for project management.

Since the beginning of private and public partnering, there have been many pioneers who are learning how to make partnering a part of their organization's culture. Partnering is still in its infancy. There will be many more pioneers who will teach us new and better ways to make partnering work. These new efforts will continue to make projects better for everyone.

In 1987 Colonel Charles Cowan of the U.S. Army Corps of Engineers and Norm Anderson of the Washington State Department of Transportation simultaneously began to develop cooperative programs for their public projects

These programs began to be called "public partnering"

---

[*]There may have been many others who started at this time, for when it's time for something to spring forth, it usually does so in many places.

"Clearly, the best dispute resolution is dispute prevention. Acting to prevent disputes before they occur is key to building new cooperative relationships. By taking the time at the start of a project to identify common goals, common interests, lines of communication, and a commitment to cooperative problem solving, we encourage the will to resolve disputes and achieve project goals."

Lieutenant General H. J. Hatch
Commander, U.S. Army Corps of Engineers
Policy Memorandum 11, 7 August 1990

7
The Foundations of Partnering

…we never attack. An attack is proof that one is out of control.
Morihei Ueshiba (1863-1969), history's greatest martial artist

There are certain foundations required for partnering. When these things are present, the partnering thrives. When they are not present, the partnering never takes off or jells.

Figure 4

There are certain foundations required for partnering — when they are present the partnering will thrive

Ownership of the Problems

Ownership of the problems means that when a problem is identified to you, you accept the problem equally, as your own. You don't tell the person to talk to someone else, or that this isn't your problem; you help them find the right person to get a quick response. Many times project members find themselves stuck in "voice-mail hell." You leave a message for the person you think you need to talk to, only to find out two days later that she isn't the right person, and you should call someone else. You call that "someone else" only to find out they are on vacation. You wait two weeks and upon their return you find out that they aren't the right person for you to talk with either. I have seen cases where several months may pass on a project before people can find out who they need to talk to about a problem. Patience has run thin, the project has moved along, and what was a minor problem has now adversely affected the critical path.

Ownership of a problem means that when a problem is identified to you, you accept the problem equally as your own.

Ownership of the problem also means that, no matter what the problem is, or who you feel "should" be responsible, you set aside assigning accountability in order to seek a resolution. You do this because experience has shown that a cooperative partnering attitude fosters the sharing of problems. Working together to solve problems also provides an opportunity to gain input from those who are less entrenched in the issues, and who may come up with a solution no one saw before. I have witnessed this several times. One team had struggled along with a problem, with no readily apparent solution acceptable to all. At a meeting an individual, not previously involved with the project, happened to be attending to see how things were going. After fifteen minutes he suggested a solution to which everyone said "of course." To him the solution was obvious, and it became obvious to everyone else once they heard it.

Working together to solve problems produces better solutions

Ownership of problems stops finger pointing and gets everyone working together to solve problems quickly. Ownership of problems does not mean that everyone will pay equally for the problems, but it does mean that everyone has the ability and commitment to lessen the impact of problems.

Full Disclosure

Full disclosure means that you tell everyone what you know. You don't hold back; you tell them the good, the bad and the ugly. The team can't make the best decision without all of the information. If you were invited to a friend's weekly Saturday night poker game, but were not told the "house rules" — which cards were always wild, that the pot limit automatically doubled after midnight, and that, by the way the jack of hearts was missing from the deck — what chance would you have of winning? Next to none.

Many times the stakeholders fail to share all the information they know about the project. They keep some of the cards to themselves. This makes it difficult to reach the best decisions. In the long-run, even difficult things are best disclosed. On one project the contractor inadvertently left a major item out of his bid. Disclosing this information at the start of construction enabled the project team to lessen the impact to the job. The owner didn't open up the checkbook to the contractor, but the team did find ways to make it less costly for the contractor, while assuring that the oversight did not stall the project. Such errors far too often develop into big battles later on in the project, when there is no opportunity to rethink approaches and create novel solutions, and by which time everyone is pointing fingers.

The project team can't make the best decision without knowing all the information

Full disclosure, then, means that you keep no hidden agendas or aces up your sleeves. You share everything you know so that together you can create ways to improve the project and solve problems. Fundamentally, you are seeking solutions, not who to blame. Experienced people realize that due to the interdependence of each project team organization on a construction project there is usually only win-win or lose-lose. Your success is tied to the success of the other stakeholders, so why not play with a full deck?

Full disclosure means no hidden agendas, no aces up your sleeves

Empower Others

A lot has been written and said about empowerment. Empowerment on your project really comes down to allowing decisions to be made at the project management level. When

DILBERT Reprinted by permission of United Feature Syndicate, Inc.

Figure 5

If you were really empowered, there wouldn't be a special phrase for it

decisions leave the project management level, they often grow into larger problems.

Most of our organizations are still hierarchical. Power resides at the top of the organization and little filters down to the bottom. This structure tends to block decision making on projects. If those in the field lack the authority to make decisions, then the project waits until those higher-up in the organization decide. This can have a devastating impact on the schedule and on project relationships. Empowerment calls for those closest to the issue, who often know the most about the issue, to be the decision makers. This gives you fast, good decisions that the field team supports.

If the field can't make decisions, then the project must wait until those higher up do — no matter how long it takes

For many organizations, public organizations in particular, empowerment is a difficult challenge. They are by nature bureaucratic with authority reserved only for the highest levels within the organization. Partnering is really counter-cultural for such organizations. A special internal effort must be made to determine how partnering will be handled within such organizations. Will the traditional levels of authority continue to exist, or can they be adjusted so that empowerment can occur at the project management level? Are there ways to streamline processes so decisions can be made faster? Bureaucratic organizations usually have to work harder to implement partnering successfully. You can't just attend a partnering workshop and go back to your organization, do everything as you always have, and expect different results. You must change.

It has been my experience that, when guided by a clear project and company/organization mission, field personnel usually will make good decisions.

Commitment

There are few guarantees in life, but I can offer you one. The partnership on your project will be as successful as your commitment to it. No more, and no less. It takes commitment to do things differently, it takes commitment to deal with people differently, and it takes commitment to look at problems from different vantage points. Think of a ham and eggs breakfast. The hen was involved, the pig was committed. Are you just involved in, or really committed to, partnering?

Ideally, partnering calls for a commitment from everyone in your organization. Over time, commitments may become blurry as things change, and your commitment may need to be refocused. Commitments are best when they are clear and have a defined time frame.

Far too often partners throw away the partnering values when one or more of their project team members does not live up to them. Such a failure by another team member does not have to be the end of your partnership. Your commitment can be sufficient to assure the success of the partnership. Although more difficult, success can be achieved even when everyone is not equally committed to partnering. It takes only one organization acting as a catalyst to start the partnering process and to keep it going. Your ability to listen, to understand, and to develop options for mutual benefit will help you to keep the partnership on track no matter what the other stakeholders are doing. It takes your commitment to the partnership and its goals, no matter what.

Partnering is counter-cultural to a bureaucratic, hierarchial organization

Of the few guarantees in life, one is that your partnership will only be as successful as your commitment to it — no more and no less

Trust

We have talked about trust many times in this book. Trust is the bedrock of partnering. Without trust, few of the benefits of partnering are possible. It is always possible to see how your partnership is going by using trust as your litmus test. If trust is high, your partnership is going well. If trust is low, or eroding, your partnership is in trouble and immediate action is needed.

Without trust few of the benefits of partnering are possible

The best way to achieve trust is by being trusting. As shown by game theory, trust begets more trust, just as distrust begets more distrust. If you start your project with trust, then the probability is high that you will receive trust in return. Trust allows for creativity, open communication, understanding, and commitment to the solutions reached.

Some people just can't bring themselves to trust. If you are such a person, then be trustworthy. Yes, it can be difficult to trust because you don't want to trust blindly and be proven wrong. Trust is often a decision, a decision not to let the past predict your future. Your old mind-set about someone, or a particular kind of organization, or a particular group, can make you feel distrustful. This is where you can make a decision, ideally to trust, at a minimum to be trustworthy, despite your past encounters. This by itself will help to build trust.

The best way to achieve trust is to be trusting

8

The Four Stages of Partnering

Different strokes for different folks

Unknown

All partnerings are not alike. In fact, no partnering workshop is exactly like any other. Every job is different. The complexity of demands of each job, mixed with the people assigned to the project and their relationships, make for different challenges on each job. Most partnerings fall into one of four stages of partnering.

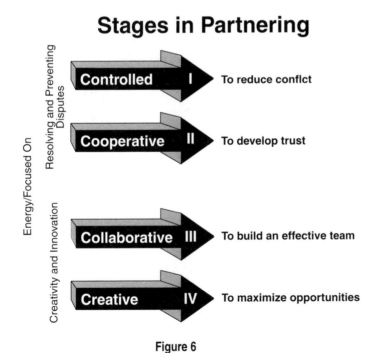

Stages in Partnering

Energy/Focused On

Resolving and Preventing Disputes

Creativity and Innovation

Controlled	I	To reduce conflct
Cooperative	II	To develop trust
Collaborative	III	To build an effective team
Creative	IV	To maximize opportunities

Figure 6

Stage One

A stage one partnering occurs when conflict erupts. Large change orders, threats, positioning letters, and frayed tempers feed each other and gain momentum. Or, you may have some combination of owner, architect, and contractor with a history of not getting along, and now these individuals are thrust together to design and/or build a project. I have witnessed several situations in which a single event occurred early on in the project that set the stage for an ongoing battle.

The focus of partnering at Stage One is to control the chaos

The focus of partnering at this stage is to control the chaos that has broken out or that is imminent. You can reduce the conflict by increasing the amount of control each party feels they have over the project. This increase in control is achieved by having the team members agree on how they will work together.

Depending upon the specific issues, the partnering team works to develop agreed-upon control systems. These may include understanding each person's role, responsibility and level of authority, defining lines of communication, and/or developing a decision making process, a dispute resolution process, or a change order process. Procedures for disseminating and requesting information also reduce the potential for conflict.

At stage one it may be necessary to develop communication skills to help deal with differences

It also may be advantageous for the team members to develop specific skills to help them deal with their differences. These skills might include listening, communicating or negotiating. A seasoned partnering facilitator will be able to identify which core skills need strengthening, and can then design an appropriate training module.

Stage Two

A stage two partnering is when the stakeholders find that they do not know each other and therefore don't know what to expect from one another. Or it may be that the stakeholders have had both positive and negative experiences with each other in the past and feel uncertain about working together again on a new project.

At this stage the partnering is focused on getting the stakeholders to know each other and on building trust so that cooperation can begin. Exhibiting your trustworthiness is critical, so it is important to develop measurable goals at the partnering session. Achieving promised goals is a concrete method of building trust.

Goals should be measurable and achievable. Wishful thinking such as having no rain during the winter months of the project, while measurable, cannot be achieved. Further, creating such a goal sets a precedent of being impractical, how can you work together to assure there is no rain? You've already failed!

Stage Two focuses on building trust and getting to know each other

Goals should be achievable in the not-too-distant future. This allows the partners to see if (and when) they are accomplished and to build up small successes. If each stakeholder does what they commit to, trust is sure to grow. Following through with the actions you commit to during the partnering workshop proves to your project partners that you can be trusted. This is a great way to start your project.

Stage Three

A third stage partnering is when the stakeholders have a history of getting along and of being successful working together. The lines between "them" and "us" are blurring. At this stage all of the stakeholders join together on the same side of the negotiating table and look at the project. The project becomes the focus, not each other. Trust is high and communication flows freely.

At Stage Three the lines between "them" and "us" are blurring — a real team is being built

Here the stakeholders share everything they know about the project (including difficult, uncomfortable, and scary things). This allows the team to truly work together to complete the project.

The partnering session is the catalyst used to pull the stakeholders into an effective team committed to the project. With a common vision and mission, the team members collaborate to achieve their shared goals.

Stage Four

At a stage four partnering the lines between organizations are very fuzzy, nearly nonexistent. "Them" and "us" are no longer relevant roles. The team shares a high level of trust, communicates openly and honestly, and is focused on the project's success. At this stage the stakeholders are looking for ways to improve the project and to maximize the opportunities that lie within the project.

At Stage Four the team is looking for ways to improve both their performance and the project

This stage is where creativity is the driving force and goals are based on seeking to achieve what some would say is the impossible. Here the team moves freely to meet new challenges, making the challenge work for the project rather than against it.

At this stage you have arrived at the point where continuous improvement is possible; indeed, it is happening. It takes this level of trust and a creative atmosphere for innovation to flourish.

A Different Approach for Different Folks

The first two stages of partnering are focused on resolving and preventing disputes

If you were to draw a line between stage two and stage three, you would discover that the first two stages of partnering have a different focus than the second two stages. In stages one and two the energy of the team is focused on resolving and preventing disputes. In stages three and four the team's energy is spent on creativity and innovation, looking for ways to improve the project.

Partnering offers a wide range of potential benefits, depending on the project, the team, and the stakeholders' history. Clearly, one cookie-cutter approach to partnering will not give you optimal results. The partnering workshop must be custom designed for your project, and for its current stage of partnering.

The second two stages of partnering are focused on creativity and innovation

It is going through the partnering process together that yields results. Just because you have previously attended partnering workshops does not mean that you will gain the collective agreements and results of a partnered project on today's project. You and this project's team must go through the partnering process together.

9

Create Options and Solutions for Mutual Gain

Compromise means 1 + 1 = 1½
Synergy means 1 + 1 = 8, or 16, or 1,600

Stephen R. Covey
7 Habits of Highly Effective People

Several months after a particular partnering workshop, one of the participants called me to complain about a teammate. He said that the teammate was not being a good partner, that "they just won't do what I say." Unfortunately, some people see partnering as calling for capitulation, or going along to get along. But partnering is not about one side just giving in, or about compromising all of the time. It is about trusting each other enough to be willing to throw tough issues on the table and wrestle with them together, seeking to understand each point of view and everyone's interests. Then, together, you can develop options for resolving the issue.

On construction projects the interests of the owner, contractor, designer, and construction manager are intertwined. Everyone knows what a successful project would be: completed on-time and within budget. With few exceptions every player's activities affect the others. If submittals are incomplete, response will be slow. If decisions are late, schedules will slide. Everything in the project is connected.

Partnering Values Grid

Figure 7

Partnering occurs when your concern for others is equal to your self-concern

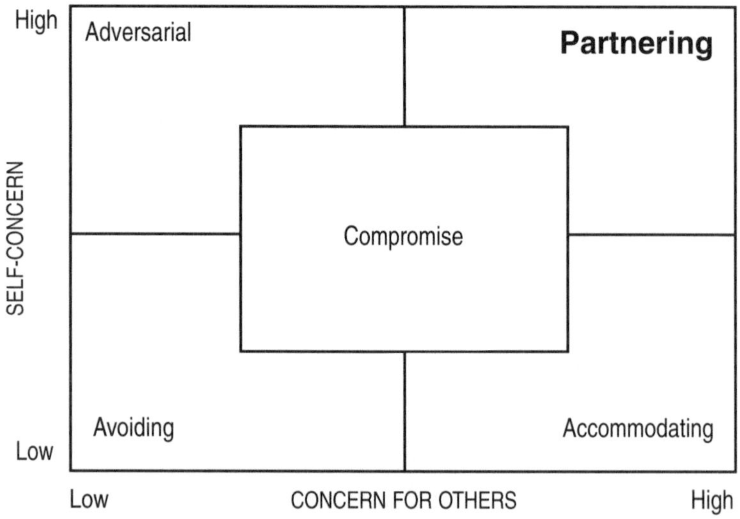

The Partnering Values Grid reveals the values upon which partnering is based. The vertical axis indicates the degree of self-concern, while the horizontal axis indicates concern for others. Today's approach to projects has become adversarial. This approach is indicated by a high concern for self-interests, and a low concern for others. In the adversarial approach I will look out for myself and my interests and I expect you to look out for your interests. We will fight it out to determine who wins, and by fighting it out we assume it will somehow be fair.

The partnering approach calls for a high concern for yourself **and** for others. It assumes that you ask for 100 percent of what you need **and** allow for 100 percent of what others need. It has been my experience that by looking for ways to give everyone what they need, 80-85 percent of the time you can figure out ways to achieve solutions which are better for everyone. Better than fighting would achieve, and better than compromising or splitting the difference would accomplish.

Compromise, while a fast way to solve problems, is not particularly creative

Compromise, as you can see in the Partnering Values Grid, is splitting the difference between all the interested parties. Compromise, although a fast way of solving problems, is not particularly creative. Working together to identify potential options and solutions will yield better results and result in a more durable agreement on how to proceed.

Avoiding conflict or making unilateral decisions indicates low concern for yourself and others. This situation occurs when people do not feel empowered to make decisions, or if the issue is one they simply don't want to deal with. Such an approach causes other parties to become more adversarial while trying to get input or a decision from the "avoiding" person.

Avoiding conflict isn't the solution; creatively resolving the inevitable conflict is

The accommodating styles of resolving problems is characterized by a high concern for others and a low concern for your own interests. In this approach the focus is going along to get along. The relationship is of foremost concern. This style is often mistaken for partnering, when, in fact, it causes resentment in those always giving in, and results in poor decisions being made.

Pushing the Envelope of Satisfaction

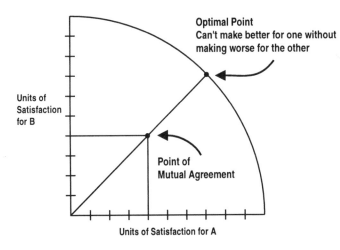

Optimal Point
Can't make better for one without making worse for the other

Units of Satisfaction for B

Point of Mutual Agreement

Units of Satisfaction for A

Figure 8

When you reach the point that making the situation better for anyone makes it worse for the others, you have an optimum solution

Our traditional way of negotiating agreements and solving problems is to make an offer. You offer 1, I say I need 8, you come back with 2 and I counter with 7. You up the ante to 3 and I offer to accept 6. You say you can't really do better than 5, and I say I'll starve unless I get 4. You say you'll give me 4 but probably will lose your job for doing so, and I lament that even if I get 4 I'll bleed to death. We have found our point of mutual agreement — the point of mutual dissatisfaction. That is, we walked away from the negotiation feeling that neither of us got what we needed. I have heard people say that it must have been a good negotiation because everyone thought it was unfair. We argued over who would get the larger piece of the existing pie, instead of trying to make the pie bigger.

It's better to work toward making a bigger pie than to fight over the pieces of a small one

But, by approaching negotiations and problem solving with a partnering approach, you can actually expand the pie for everyone. By understanding what each party needs, and creating solutions and options that will meet those needs, you can increase the level of satisfaction for everyone. This is especially true for construction projects where so many of the interests of the stakeholders are overlapping.

The solution you reach by using the partnering approach may not be exactly in the center (the optimal point) as indicated on the figure, but it will be better than if you limit the pie of possibilities to its smallest size. Partnering allows you to make better decisions for the benefit of the project and for the stakeholders.

10

Building a Shadow Organization

The single greatest cause for the failure of communism was that communism was organized based on the bureaucratic model.

Kenneth Johnston
Busting Bureaucracy

Lines of Communication

A construction project brings together many different organizations. Each one brings with it its unique organizational culture, interests, ways of doing business, processes, and rituals. All of these differences can create a clash of the titans. Communication becomes a challenge as the number of organizations grows, and as the different lines of communication which must be kept open also grow.

Complexity Grows as More People Become Involved

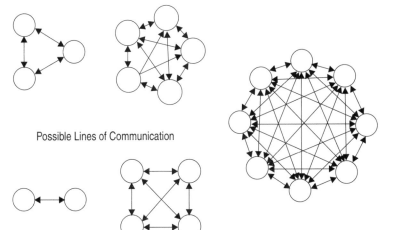

As the number of organizations grows, communications becomes a challenge

Possible Lines of Communication

Figure 9

This complexity increases exponentially when you consider the differences among the cultures of the organizations and the personalities and experiences of the people who come together to build a project. Developing a shadow organization (see figure 11) is a way to manage this complexity.

Developing a shadow organization is a way to deal with the differences between organizations

The figure below indicates the number of lines necessary for one-on-one communication as the number of parties grows. Managing such communication takes a concerted effort. Partnering offers a way to foster the free flow of information , ideas, and problems.

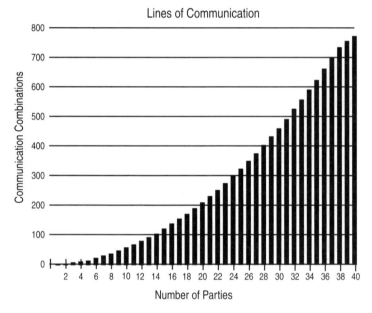

Lines of Communication

Figure 10

An organization is a group of people who have a shared mission, goals, and values

Developing a Shadow Organization Dedicated To The Project

What is an organization? It is a group of people who share a mission, goals, and values. It exists to accomplish its mission and goals while being directed by its values.

Partnering brings together all of the critical organizations associated with a project. This includes the owner, general contractor and key subcontractors, the designers, and often a construction manager. All of these different organizations

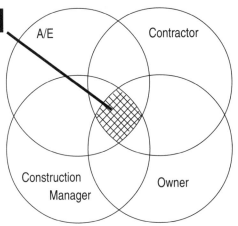

SHADOW ORGANIZATION

Your Partnering Team develops its own: mission, goals, values

Each organization has its own:
Organizational culture
Interests
Paradigms

Figure 11

work together during the partnering session to develop an agreed-upon mission and goals and commit to using partnering values to guide their work on the project. This is, by definition, an organization. The partnering team has become a new and distinct organization dedicated to working together to build a project. This shadow organization's mission and goals are based on the common interests of all the project team members. These overlapping interests are indicated as the shaded area of the figure above. This new shadow organization can work in the shadows of all the parent organizations, seeking to accomplish its mission and goals through the use of shared values. This shadow organization is committed to doing whatever it takes within each of the stakeholder organizations to ensure its mission is accomplished.

The partnering team is a new, distinct organization dedicated to working together to build a project

By working in the shadow of their own organization, the partnering team members need not run counter to the culture of their organizations. This permits flexibility and creativity in the shadow organization's efforts to accomplish its mission. Everyone wins.

Building small empowered teams which are not constrained by current organizational culture is the way of the future, and may be the only way to truly change some organizational cultures. A partnering team offers an opportunity to begin to experience a more flexible approach, which can then help the entire organization deal with change more effectively.

Small empowered teams, unconstrained by current organizational culture, are the way of the future.

11

What Partnering is Not

I hate definitions.

Benjamin Disraeli

We've talked a lot about what partnering is and how to make it work for your project. But it is important to also talk about what partnering is not.

Partnering is Not a Legal Agreement

When you sign the partnering agreement (or charter) at the end of the partnering workshop, it is not a legal document. It is your personal commitment to the mission, goals, dispute process, evaluation process and partnering values. It is also a commitment on the part of your organization to work to achieve the partnering objectives. The intent is not to create a binding document, but rather to develop a collective agreement and expectation for working together on the project.

A partnering agreement is not a legal document; it is a personal commitment

Partnering is Not a Substitute for Any Law or Regulations

Partnering is not a substitute for the construction contract or for the laws and regulations under which the contract was issued. All of the laws, regulations and contract documents stay intact. Partnering seeks to develop a good working relationship so that as you execute the contract, complying with the laws and regulations upon which it is based, you will gain a better understanding and agreement on how to cooperatively administer the construction contract.

Partnering is not a substitute for the construction contract, laws, or documents

Partnering is Not a Waiver of Rights by Anyone

You and your partners do not give up any of your rights because you partner a project. While partnering seeks to find mutually beneficial outcomes to disputes, it does not preclude any party from seeking legal, political or other means of resolving disputes. It does not mean that you must do what others tell you because you are "partners." As has been stated before, partnering is not about going along to get along.

Partnering seeks to find mutually beneficial outcomes to disputes

Partnering is Not an Excuse to Not Perform

Partnering is not an excuse to fail to perform top-quality work. Just because you are partners, you can't expect others to automatically forgive you your mistakes, problems, or failures. Working together you can try to find ways to lessen their impact, however, you are still responsible to perform your duties on the project.

Partnering is not an excuse to fail to perform top quality work

Partnering is Not a Guarantee There Won't be Disagreements or Problems

Disagreements occur on almost every project. It doesn't mean that your partnership is a failure if disagreements arise. It does mean that you will have a greater challenge to keep the partnering spirit alive, and to work together to find solutions to the challenges you face. Problems are the nature of construction. Dealing with the unknown factors on a project is what attracts many people to the industry. Solving problems quickly, fairly, creatively, and with less conflict is what partnering is all about.

Your partnership isn't a failure if disagreements arise

Partnering is Not a License to Expect Something for Nothing

Your partnering relationship is based on being fair with one another. Expecting someone to perform work for free, overlook a problem, or change a rule falls under the false belief that "if you were a good partner you would do it for me." Such an attitude creates resentment, erodes trust, and leads to a defensive posture by one or more of the project partners. Partnering is about working together to solve problems and negotiating a fair way of assessing risk and reward.

Partnering is Not a Hammer with which to Manipulate Your Partners

Unfortunately some people try to use partnering as a hammer against their project partners. Several of the aforementioned attitudes are examples of this, and have resulted in some owners, contractors, agencies, and construction management firms being reluctant to partner. This is such an important point that I must state it once again. Partnering is NOT about giving in to what someone else wants you to do just because you are partnering your project. This expectation has done a lot to undermine the partnering process on many jobs. As a project partner you have the ability to communicate and seek to understand problems, work together to solve problems, develop alternative solutions, and fairly assess the value of each solution.

It is unfortunate that some people try to use partnering as a hammer against their project partners

PART 3

Five Steps to Partnering Your Project

STEP ONE

DECIDE: DO WE PARTNER, OR NOT?

12
Selecting a Project

The difficulty in life is the choice.

George Moore, *Bending of the Bough*

Deciding whether or not to partner a project can sometimes be challenging. To make it easier Step One will take you through a process to help you decide if and how partnering might help your project.

How Satisfied Are You?

Many people who have been in the building and construction industry for thirty to forty years tell me that partnering isn't anything new, that it is the way they used to work on projects years ago. They shook hands and went to work, accepting each other's word that they would perform.

Since then, times have changed. We can no longer simply accept the word of our fellow project team members. Building and construction have gotten more and more complex over the years as layers of regulation, bureaucracy, and liabilities have been placed on top of even the smallest projects.

What about your experience? How satisfied are you with the outcome of your projects? Are you satisfied by a job well done at the end? Could they be more successful?

EXERCISE:

Your Ideal Project

This exercise will help you imagine what you would like your projects to be like in order to be successful. Please think of a project you are considering partnering. In the space provided, write down all the ideas that come to your mind that would make this an "ideal" project. These ideas must be possible (i.e. we can't control the weather). However, exclude only the verifiably impossible - write down all the other ideas, no matter how outlandish they seem at first. This is important since many times we get stuck in our current way of seeing things.

Project: _____

If this project could be any way you wanted, what would it be like?

What would make your project ideal?

No matter how outlandish, write down every idea that would make your project ideal

Place an X next to those things you feel are most important for this project. Think of what your project would be like if it had these attributes. Would this be a great project?

The Benefits of Partnering

According to The Associated General Contractors of America's book *Partnering, Changing Attitudes in Construction*[13], the benefits derived from partnering include:

- Lower Administrative Costs
- More Innovation
- Fewer Cost Overruns
- Expedited Decision-making
- Potential to Expedite Projects
- Better Quality
- Reduced Exposure to Litigation
- Greater Opportunity for Financial Success

Compare the benefits of a partnered project to your ideal project — you'll find a great deal of similarity

Another benefit of partnering your project according to Joe Browne of Caltrans is that it establishes a relationship of mutual trust which carries far beyond the current project. The initial results are lower project costs, but the long-term effects are even more dramatic as project partnering builds on itself and leads to even more tangible results.

Compare these benefits with your ideal project: the ability to finish your project on time, within budget, with no accidents, no unresolved claims, and with a sense of satisfaction and achievement. This is the potential partnering offers your project.

Deciding When to Partner

Partnering can occur at any stage of your project's life — in the planning/environmental stage, or in the design, construction, or post-construction phases. Partnering most often takes place at the beginning of construction, although more and more owners see the benefits of beginning the process much earlier. I also have seen partnering used to get regulatory agencies to agree on a course of action so that a project could go forward. Frequently there is more than one owner on a project; or more than one entity that thinks it is the owner. An example is a highway interchange improvement project where the taxing authority (i.e. a county transportation agency or an assessment district) sees itself

Partnering can occur at any stage of your project's life

as owner because it is paying the bills, while the state's department of transportation sees itself as the owner because it will end up with the project after it is built. Tenant improvement projects are another example since one entity builds the project and a different one occupies it. Partnering helps to define agreed-upon roles and responsibilities, relieving some of the confusion caused by multiple owners. Partnering also might be considered on a project which is underway but which has developed some real problems, such as large claims or schedule slippages. Partnering can help get the project back on track.

The partnering time-benefit curve demonstrates that it is most advantageous to start partnering as soon as possible, when you have the greatest ability to influence the final cost, having the entire project's lifetime to work with. The sooner you start, the sooner you get people with construction experience and knowledge involved, the more time you have to develop a good working relationship, to adjust to changes, and to innovate to make the project better. How satisfied are you with the outcome of your projects? How satisfied are you with the outcome of your projects? How satisfied are you with the outcome of your projects?

> *It is most advantageous to start partnering as soon as possible — when you have the greatest ability to influence the project's final cost*

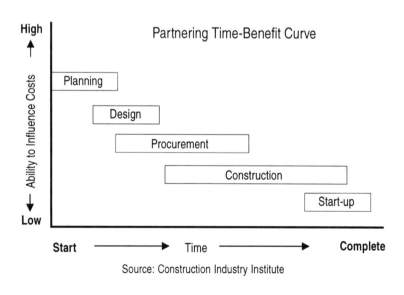

Source: Construction Industry Institute

Figure 12

13

Identifying Key Project Stakeholders

stakeholder (stak'hŏl'der) n. One who has a share or an interest, as in an enterprise.

The American Heritage College Dictionary

Identifying all the stakeholders for your project is an important task. A stakeholder is anyone who has an interest in, or may be affected by, your project. Through understanding the stakeholders, their roles, and probable objectives, you gain vast insight into the potential opportunities available to your project as well as the problems your project faces. Project stakeholders might include:

A stakeholder is anyone who has an interest in, or may be affected by, your project

The End-User

This is the group which will ultimately use the facility that is built. It may be a hospital staff, the traveling public, a library staff and patrons, or the shopping center's anchor tenant and its customers. The end user is often not present at the partnering session, but must be kept clearly in mind.

The Owner

The end user is often not present at the partnering session, but must be clearly kept in mind

The owner is the person or group(s) who will ultimately hold legal title or ownership of the project. This is sometimes the user, but often is not. Except in the case where there is a separate funding source or agency, the owner is the party who pays the bill for the project, regardless of whether it's a public or private project. The owner is ultimately responsible for ensuring that it gets the project that it is paying for in terms of quality, function, timeliness, etc.

The Funding Source

Sometimes there is a separate funding source or agency. This might be a bank, investors, a trust fund, or a special agency set up to fund projects. The funding source, naturally, is trying to manage the risk of losing its investment, or having its money spent unwisely. Confusion will occur if the funding source believes itself to be the owner. This confusion will result in a power struggle between the funding source and the real owner (the entity to whom title is transferred at the end of the job). Ironically, this conflict increases the risk of the funding source losing its investment.

The Architect

Responsible for the design of the project, the architect works diligently with the owner and user to understand the need for the project and to create a design accordingly. The architect leads the design team. The architect is responsible for delivering a design that meets the needs of the owner and the user.

Confusion will occur if the funding source believes itself to be the owner

The Engineer

On engineering projects, it is the engineer rather than the architect who is responsible for the design of the project and for working to meet the needs of the owner and the user. For building projects, the engineer works under the architect, wanting to meet the architect's needs as well as the needs of the user and the owner.

The Construction Manager

An outside firm that specializes in managing construction projects is sometimes hired by the owner to help assure the project's success. This is the construction manager. The construction manager may play a different role from project to project, depending on the relationship with the owner. The construction manager may act as an advisor, an agent, or as the general contractor.

The General Contractor

Regardless of whether the project delivery system is low bid, a negotiated contract, or design/build, the general contractor is responsible for the construction of the project and will oversee all of the work performed by its subcontractors.

The Subcontractors

On many projects subcontractors perform most of the actual construction, with the general contractor working in a role as coordinator and manager. Subcontractors will seek to make their portion of the project successful.

Because of their potential to impact the project, consider inviting your suppliers to the partnering

The Suppliers

Because the delivery of materials usually has a significant impact on schedule and budget, suppliers are critical to the project. The success of the project depends greatly on the ability of the suppliers to perform.

Regulatory Agencies

It is likely that many regulatory agencies will have a part in your project. Often they don't have any responsibility to see that the project is built, but they do have the authority to shut the project down or cause project delays. Identifying all relevant regulatory agencies and understanding their needs and requirements is an important step in assuring the success of your project.

Regulatory agencies often have no responsibility to see that the project is built — only the authority to keep them from being built

The Community

More and more communities are demanding a say in what projects are built and where they are built. If a project is to be built in a community that is not in favor of it, the community members can place enormous pressure on the project. Bringing the community, or its representatives, into the project and making them a part of the project is sometimes the only way to have it go forward.

Who Should Attend?

Keeping in mind the project you are considering partnering (from the last chapter), list all of the project's stakeholders. You may not know specific names at this time, only categories, but that's fine. Also identify what you believe to be their role and stake in your project.

List Your Project Stakeholders:

Identify all of the stakeholders involved in your project

<table>
<tr><td>

EXERCISE:

</td></tr>
</table>

Name/Category

_____	_____
_____	_____
_____	_____
_____	_____
_____	_____
_____	_____
_____	_____
_____	_____

Which of the stakeholders are key to the project's success?

Now go back over your list and place a "1" next to those stakeholders who are key to the project's success, place a "2" next to those who are important, and a "3" next to those who can have an impact but are not critical.

14

The Partnering Potential Indicator

Vision is the art of seeing things invisible.

Jonathan Swift

The Partnering Potential Indicator (PPI) is a tool to help you decide whether or not to partner a particular project. It is based on my experience in working on hundreds of projects ranging in size from $400,000 to $2.5 billion and measures the risk of potential disputes.

Please respond to each statement, indicating whether you feel that you strongly agree, strongly disagree, or are somewhere in between. Keep your project in mind as you answer each question. Your first reaction is most accurate; spending time analyzing will give you less accurate results. Enter your scores as follows:

The PPI will help you evaluate the risk of potential disputes on your project

Strongly Agree	1
Agree	1.5
Neither Agree nor Disagree	2
Disagree	2.5
Strongly Disagree	3

EXERCISE:

The test begins on the next page and consists of 33 statements. Enter your reaction to how each statement applies to your project in the box to the right of the statement. When you are finished, add up the scores for all 33 statements and enter them into the "total" box.

Score

1 Strongly Agree		

	Project:	
1	You don't know the people you will be working with	
2	The design is complex	
3	There is a history of personality conflicts	
4	The contract documents are poor	
5	There is a significant poWer imbalance between two or more organizations	
6	There are many different organizations working on this project	
7	The construction is complex	
8	Some of the people are inexperienced	
9	Cooperation of others is needed for success	
10	You are concerned about the performance of one or more stakeholders	
11	The project is rushed, pre-planning is minimal	
12	There are servere budget constraints	
13	There is a history of disputes	
14	A third party poses a significant threat	
15	One or more of the orgnanizations has a bureaucratic orgnaizational culture	
16	There is a significant potential for changed conditions	

1 Strongly Agree

1.5 Agree

2 Neither Agree nor Disagree

2.5 Disagree

3 Strongly Disagree

17	The project is politically visible or challenging	
18	The roles and responsiblities for all stakeholders is not clear/understood	
19	Time is critical	
20	A supplier(s) is critical to success	
21	There are potential environmental issues	
22	Site conditions are a challenge	
23	This is a large project for you	
24	Stakeholder(s) may be unresponsive to problems	
25	Documents may not be interpreted fairly	
26	Another stakeholder is not a team player	
27	Payments may not be prompt	
28	There is no strong leadership	
29	The scope of work is unclear or inaccurate	
30	One or more of the stakeholders is inexperienced with this type of project	
31	You have never worked together before	
32	You are not concerned about a long-term relationship	
33	There are no opportunities in this project you would like to explore	
	TOTAL	

1	Strongly Agree
1.5	Agree
2	Neither Agree nor Disagree
2.5	Disagree
3	Strongly Disagree

How to Interpret Your Partnering Potential Score

If your score is between:

90 - 99　Your project appears to have a **small risk of conflict** and problems. Partnering offers your project an opportunity for greater innovation and creativity, and a chance to achieve improved understanding, agreement and coordination.

80 - 89　There is **some risk to your project's success.** Partnering can help reduce this risk by examining each challenge and planning for its management. You also will have an opportunity to gain an understanding of what each stakeholder needs so you can better execute the project.

70 - 79　Partnering offers your project a significant benefit. You **have substantial risks to your success,** and working through some of these challenges will significantly increase your chances for success.

33 - 69　Your project has enormous benefit to be gained from partnering. Your project has many challenges that are best faced as a team. You face a **significant threat of conflict, communication, and relationship problems.**

Copy the PPI and have others in your organization use it to assess your project

Whether or not you should pursue partnering your project is indicated by your total score. If your score is 79 or below, the focus of your partnering will be to resolve and prevent disputes (see Chapter 7, The Four Stages of Partnering). Partnering will be an important and valuable tool to manage the risks you face.

If your score is 80 or above, the focus of your partnering will be creativity and innovation. Partnering can improve your project by opening up communication, building consensus and fostering innovation. You and your potential partners must decide.

I suggest that you copy the PPI and have three to five people in your organization use it to assess your project. Then, sit down together and discuss the scores to decide if you want to partner the project. If the answer is yes, then you need to prepare internally before you can persuade the other key stakeholders to partner with you.

15

Getting Ready Internally

Whether you think you can or you think you can't, you're right.

Henry Ford

It Takes Senior Management's Commitment

Partnering must become a part of your organization's business strategy to have the best chance of working. Webster's dictionary defines strategy as "a plan or method for obtaining a specific result." Partnering is the method, and an improved product is the desired result. While partnering requires commitment from all levels in the organization, it must have senior management's sincere backing to become a true business strategy.

Top management's attitude makes an enormous difference. You need at least one key person in senior management to champion partnering within your organization. If you are not a part of senior management, it may fall upon you to educate your senior management so they understand some of the potential benefits of partnering. Part I described in depth the potential benefits of partnering.

If you are a part of senior management, it is important that you understand the benefits of partnering and, even more important, that you show your commitment to it. Your organization needs to learn what partnering means to it. There is a learning curve. It takes some time to learn how to opti-

Top management's attitude makes a tremendous difference — you need at least one key person in senior management to champion partnering within your organization

mize the new relationships. The work you do prior to starting the partnering process will go a long way in helping your organization to be ready.

There is no better indication of your commitment to partnering than your full-time attendance at the partnering session — actions speak louder than words. It is also up to you to make sure your on-site people are committed to, and remain committed to, the partnership.

For partnering to have significant, continuing results, the project team must walk-the-partnering-talk every day

EXERCISE:

Who is (or do you want to be) your Senior Management Partnering Champion(s)?

_____   _____

Examine Barriers to Partnering

The most significant barrier to partnering is that YOU MUST CHANGE

There are several barriers to successful partnering, such as gaining senior management's commitment, developing an attitude of openness and honesty, and examining any misalignment of values. Another barrier is the mistaken belief that partnering is a one-time event (the partnering workshop). Many people become disillusioned when, after a successful partnering workshop where everyone agrees to a shared vision and common goals and objectives, things on the project improve for only a short period of time. For partnering to have significant, continuing results, the project team must walk-the-partnering-talk every day.

The most significant barrier to partnering is that in order to partner effectively with several other organizations, YOU MUST CHANGE. Change is hard for most people and organizations. It means you must rethink how you do things, challenge the status quo, and become flexible in your approach to people and problems. If you attend a partnering workshop, and you change nothing from how you have operated in the past, either internally or externally, then you will not improve your project. If you continue doing what you have been doing, you will continue getting the same results. And since you are trying to improve your project, you must do some things in new ways.

Review Internal Processes

Looking at internal processes can help you understand how you currently operate, and see where you can build in more flexibility. There are three main areas to target.

Because empowerment is one of the primary goals/ values of partnering, successful partnering will be far more difficult in a hierarchy

Hierarchy
If your organization is structured with the highest authority at the top and greatly decreasing authority as you go down the organizational chart, then your organization is a hierarchy. A hierarchy by definition is bureaucratic. It may be a small or large bureaucracy, but either way, a hierarchy blocks empowerment of individuals. Because empowerment is one of the primary goals/values of partnering, successful partnering will be far more difficult in a hierarchy. I have found that it is possible to create a project team separate from the rest of the organization, and allow it to work outside the normal chain-of-command, within a new structure developed just for the project (see Chapter 10).

Decision-making
Making the best decisions in the least amount of time is critical to your project's success. The decision-making process can be slower when it is unclear who is the decision-maker or when there are many decision-makers who individually review and comment on each issue before it is returned for a final decision. Concurrent review and decision-making allow for faster, better responses. Again, your organization's structure may hamper your decision-making process, so review your processes for various types of decisions and see if you can streamline them, if not throughout the organization, then on the project.

Don't assume two people within the same organization share the same knowledge; many times it's easier to communicate across organizations than within them

Information Flow
Information and communication are the lifeblood of your project. Information must flow freely within your organization and between your project team members. Understanding how information flows can help you design new, better

ways in which to transmit and communicate information. Don't assume that two project partners know the same information just because they belong to the same organization; many times internal power struggles keep information away from one group. Carefully examine your organization's information and communication flows. Redesign them as necessary; don't let "this is how we have always done it" dictate how your project's information flows.

For partnering to work effectively you must align the values of your organization with those of partnering

Align Your Organization with Partnering Values

Aligning the values of your organization with those of partnering is of paramount importance if partnering is to work effectively. For example, if you "partner" a project without really valuing input from the other project stakeholders, project communication will become a problem. If information and authority are closely held commodities within your organization, how can you expect to have open and honest communication with your partners? Partnering values need to be integrated into all parts of your organization and into your culture. Some of the key values of partnering include:

- Cooperation
- Trust
- Open and Honest Communication
- Teamwork
- Fairness
- Joint Problem-solving
- Working for Mutual Gain
- Rapid Dispute Resolution at the Field Level

How do your organization's values compare to partnering's?

EXERCISE:

How does your organization rate on all of these values? Are they a part of how you operate now, or are they different from your current norms? If they are different, how are you going to make them a part of your organization?

_____

_____

_____

_____

_____

_____

Reward the behavior you wish to encourage

_____

_____

_____

_____

_____

_____

Reward People

The reward for partnering can take many forms; it doesn't have to be monetary

To truly show your commitment to the partnering concepts, you must reward those who show their willingness and commitment to partnering. Many contractors have made safety a part of their business strategy. Project managers are paid a bonus based on many things, one of which is their project's safety record. The reward for partnering can take many forms; it doesn't have to be monetary (which is difficult for public agencies). A reward can be a plaque, senior management's personal recognition, an article in your local paper or in-house publication, or a dinner on the town. It doesn't matter what it is; what matters is that you are demonstrating your commitment to partnering. If you don't re-ward those who are willing to make an effort to make your partnership work, you have, by default, demonstrated your lack of commitment to partnering.

Now that you have decided whether or not to partner and have begun to get ready internally, you are ready to enlist the other key project stakeholders.

STEP TWO

ENLIST KEY PROJECT STAKEHOLDERS

16

Selling the Concept

A clever, imaginative, humorous request can open closed doors and closed minds.

Percy Ross

Inviting The Project Team To Partner

Architects, engineers and owners are best positioned to consider partnering their project from its inception, but the desire to partner is certainly not limited to them. Often it takes the contractor's excitement and commitment to partnering to enlist the owner and architect. If you feel that partnering is a valuable tool for your project, then it is your responsibility to sell the other project stakeholders.

Approaching the other project members works best if you consider their points of view, showing them that you have considered their needs. Also effective is showing them results from third parties; doing so will add credibility and objectivity to your dialogue.

If you feel that partnering is a valuable tool for your project, then it is your responsibility to sell the other project stakeholders

Finding Common Ground

Looking at your project from another's point of view can be accomplished through the following exercise.

EXERCISE:

Write down to which of your project stakeholders you are going to "sell" the partnering concept (owner, funding agency, architect/engineer, construction manager, contractor, supplier, regulatory agency). Now list what you believe to be their project objectives. Remember to approach this from their point of view.

_____   _____

_____   _____

_____   _____

_____   _____

_____   _____

_____   _____

_____   _____

_____   _____

Showing others third-party testimonials confirming the positive results of partnering will greatly assist your effort

Which of these objectives are the same or similar to your own project objectives? The ones that you have just identified are your common ground. Those objectives which are different may be best addressed in the open atmosphere of a partnering workshop.

Now repeat this exercise for each project stakeholder you need to approach and sell on partnering your project.

Third Party Results and Information

This book has been designed for you to give to your prospective partners as a gift or for them to use as a tool

Showing your project stakeholders third-party testimonials confirming the positive results of partnering will greatly assist your effort.

This book has been designed for you to give to your prospective partners as a gift or for them to use as a tool. It will help them understand partnering, the potential benefits for everyone involved, and how to make it work for your project. Encourage them to utilize the Partnering Potential Indicator (PPI) (Chapter 14). After they have completed the

PPI work sheet, schedule a time to meet with them to discuss the results.

The Construction Industry Institute is a nonprofit organization whose membership is comprised of both public and private owners. CII sponsors research targeted toward improving the construction process. The organization is continually doing benchmarking studies on the results of partnering. The most recent study at the time of this book's writing, done in 1995, showed the following results for public works projects:

Eighty-eight percent of those surveyed were satisfied with their partnering relationship

Example of Improvements in Public Sector Projects from Partnering - CII Data, 1995		
	Partnering	Traditional
Number of Projects	16	36
Contract Amount	$160mm	$400mm
Average Project Size	$10mm	$11.1mm
Cost of Changes	2.5%	16.5%
Duration of Changes	8.1%	18.2%
Change Order Costs	3.9%	15.2%
Claim Costs	0.01%	7.7%
Value Engineering	4.2%	0.4%

Source: CII

Figure 13

CII also conducted a four-year benchmarking study on partnering which was released in 1994.

Are you satisfied with your partnering relationship?

Will partnering's use increase or stay the same?

Source: CII News, September, 1994

Figure 14

Sixty-nine percent of those surveyed thought that the use of partnering will increase

85

Source and Amount of Savings on Total Installed Cost			
Value Engineering	4.00%	Reduced Inspection and Administrative Work	1.80%
Reduced Re-work	6.25%	Schedule Savings	7.90%

Figure 15

CII's efforts are ongoing, so you will want to keep up on its latest research results. You can contact CII for a free catalog which lists the most recent partnering research documents:

The Construction Industry Institute
The University of Texas at Austin
3208 Red River
Suite 300
Austin, TX 78705-2650
(512) 471-4319
FAX (512) 499-8101

You can contact the Construction Industry Institute for a catalog listing the latest partnering research documents

Design Professionals Insurance Companies (DPIC) has found partnering to be so beneficial for their design clients that under their PARTNERED TEAM COVER they will pay for partnering on their client's projects. They have produced a video tape titled *On Time, On Budget* which can be obtained by calling DPIC at (800) 227-8533.

The Associated General Contractors of America has published a book titled *Partnering, Changing Attitudes in Construction*. It includes many case studies which you can share as specific examples with your prospective partners. To order call AGC of America at (202) 393-2040.

They Don't Have to be Sold, Just Willing to Try

Your job is to get them to the partnering workshop — your facilitator will create the right atmosphere

You don't have to completely sell them on the idea of partnering; just attain their willingness to try. Getting their commitment to come to the workshop, and agreeing that there may be a way to improve the project by working together, is enough. Your professional partnering facilitator will then help create the right atmosphere and process to bring everyone together. Your job is to get them there.

17

Overcoming Objections

Others have seen what is and asked why. I have seen what could be and asked why not.

Robert F. Kennedy

Partnering is a voluntary process, but sometimes in order to get started it is necessary to overcome objections others throw at you about partnering. Remember, people are usually resistive to change, and partnering is a different way of approaching a project. When people raise objections they are usually asking for more information or for some control.

When people give you objections, don't try to convince them; they will be much more likely to argue with you and distrust your motives. Instead, find a third-party endorsement, someone to help explain their viewpoint of partnering, and why, in their opinion, the objection is not valid. Third-party endorsements should be from someone the objector respects, and can be in the form of written articles, a phone call, a video presentation, a conference call, a personal letter, research results, or anything you can think of that will help answer their objection.

Your job is to lead by asking questions and to seek to understand what it is they're objecting to. Continue to ask questions that will move them toward giving partnering a try. Remember, they don't have to be sold on partnering, just willing to give it a try. This process will feel uncomfortable at first, but remember that you are seeking to understand rather than to convince, and you can get help from others

Remember, partnering represents a change and people are usually resistive of change

Your job is to lead by asking questions that will move them toward giving partnering a try

who can present their point of view, and you can obtain third-party endorsements. If the stakeholder remains unwilling, you will be unable to partner your project. If you really believe that partnering is important for your project, then you must get your key project stakeholders on-board.

The following are commonly heard objections to partnering, and what you might say (or get someone else to say) in response.

If after all your efforts the stakeholder remains unwilling, you will be unable to partner your project — partnering is a voluntary process

We already partner

- Tell me more; how do you partner now?
- Do you think the other project stakeholders do the same?
- Is this project important to your organization?
- Do you think meeting everyone, and getting to know each other a bit better, would help us work together more effectively?
- That's what I think, too; partnering can be a tool to help us do just that.
- Do you think it's worth a try?

I don't like "touchy-feely" stuff

- What kinds of things are "touchy-feely"?
- Yeah, I know what you mean, I felt the same way until I went to a partnering workshop and it wasn't anything like that.
- What if we made sure we didn't do anything like that at OUR workshop?
- What kinds of things would you see as beneficial for our project?
- Are you willing to work with me to make sure we develop the type of workshop we want?

Answer objections with questions

We don't have the time, we have to push, we're already behind

- How do you think we can improve on the way we spend our time (schedule)?
- That sounds like it has merit; how might we go about making that happen?

- What do you think will happen if everyone doesn't agree?
- Do you think it would be beneficial to get everyone working together to make this happen?
- Yeah, it does seem critical. I found a partnering workshop the best way to bring us all together quickly, and build consensus around such a critical issue.
- I am willing to jump on this and help you get it going. When do you want to do it?

It's too expensive

- What do you think our partnering might cost? (See if they understand the true cost, and which cost they are referring to; it might be time disguised as expense)
- Have you ever had a job that went sour?
- Wouldn't it be worth it to keep that from happening to our project?
- Partnering has a good track record for preventing disputes, and helping communication flow; how about if we explore it together, and see if we can find a way to make it cost effective for our project?

If you think partnering is too expensive, just think how expensive not partnering could be

We tried that before, and it didn't work

- When did you try partnering, and what happened?
- What do you think contributed to its failure?
- Do you think that might happen on our project?
- Do you think if everyone at least got to know each other, and knew who to talk to, it would help?
- How about trying partnering again, and we can work together to assure those things don't happen on our project?

It's too late, this project is already underway (or in trouble)

It's never too late to try partnering

- Can you tell me why you think it is too late to try partnering?
- How do you think things might be improved?
- Do you think we understand what the problems (or potential problems) are?

- Do you feel that communication is flowing well, (especially now that there are real problems)?
- Do you think that partnering now might help us get control of our project?
- How about if we work together to set up a session that meets our needs?

This project is too small; partnering is for large, complex jobs

- How large do you feel a project should be for partnering to work?
- What kinds of potential problems do you think might occur on our project?
- Wouldn't you like to head those problems off before they have a chance to really impact us?
- I would be willing to give it a try, and together we can set up a partnering workshop to make sure we stay on track. How about it?

You also could give them a copy of this book which includes the Partnering Potential Indicator, which can help them see where potential benefits can be derived. Or, you can show them your copy and explain what you see as potential benefits.

Many times what people state as their objection is not their true objection. The questions above will help you explore what their real objections are, and what their real needs are. Then you can help them fulfill their needs, address their true objectives, and show them how partnering is important for your project.

Often I am called upon by clients to explain to one of their project's stakeholders what partnering is, what it is not, and how it works. Understanding the answers to those questions helps everyone make a decision together as to whether they want to proceed.

One way to overcome objections is to give them a copy of this book

Many times the stated objection is not the true concern — by listening to the answers to your questions you can determine the real objection

18
Deciding Who Will Pay

The future is purchased by the present
THE ROAD TO SUCCESS is Always Under Construction

Deciding who will pay for your partnering session is often the first agreement that is made by your partnering team. Payment can be made in several different ways, but because it is so important to have each key stakeholder "buy-in" to the partnering process, I recommend that the key stakeholders share the cost of the partnering. This assures the commitment of each, and makes them each an equal player. If one stakeholder pays for the entire cost, the others may feel less power to make decisions and to express viewpoints. This can be detrimental for your partnership. Additionally, it may cause the facilitator to be viewed as being "associated" with the paying party, decreasing the facilitator's effectiveness as a neutral later on in the project. If one stakeholder ends up paying the entire cost, then the resulting power imbalance must be managed.

The first agreement to be reached by your partnering team is who will pay, and how

The division of payment also must be seen as fair by all stakeholders. If one feels he is being taken advantage of, your partnership can be hurt. So understanding the constraints on some organizations is important. For example, a public entity may not have separate funds available for partnering, but can use a change order to fund the session through the contractor. The contractor may feel that since the cost of a partnering session was not included as a bid item he shouldn't have to pay. Or, you may run into the situation where the members of a public agency are not allowed to have a contractor "buy them lunch" at a partnering session

Understanding the constraints on some organizations is important

- each person being required to pay for his own meal. By understanding any constraints, you can determine a fair method for sharing costs and responsibilities among all of the stakeholders. It is essential that you always make an effort to ensure you have buy-in, commitment, and fairness. The following are some ideas to help.

Buy-In

Buy-in can also be obtained by "sweat equity"

Buy-in can be obtained not only through the ritual of paying for your fair share of the costs of a partnering workshop, but also through sweat equity. A partner with financial constraints can perform some of the many tasks required to have a successful partnering. They might send out the invitations and directions to the stakeholders, set up the meeting place and arrange for food, confirm the attendance of the stakeholders, distribute the reports after the workshop, volunteer to organize follow-up sessions, or anything else that needs to be done to support the partnership. Obtaining such buy-in is especially important for stakeholders who volunteer to pay for the entire workshop because they feel partnering is important to them. They must create ways to allow others to buy-in and feel like equal partners.

Commitment

Commitment can appear in many forms, but regardless of the form, it is essential to successful partnering

Partnering takes commitment. Starting out by showing your commitment, and securing commitment from the other key stakeholders can mean the difference between a whole-hearted effort and a lukewarm effort at partnering. Commitment can appear in many forms. It might be flexibility in arranging the date, time and place for your workshop. It might be a willingness to financially support the partnering effort, or spend time sharing with your entire project team what partnering is, the commitments that you have made to partnering, and how each member of the project is an important part of the effort.

Commitment also means following through on what you say you will do; in other words, keeping your commitments. This, above all else, will begin to build trust, and trust is the foundation for your partnership.

Fairness

Fairness is a fundamental value in partnering. Start off by assuring fairness in the setup of your partnering workshop. This can go a long way toward instilling this value in the key stakeholders. When someone pays more than they feel is their fair share, trust is eroded, resentment arises, and people begin to keep score. Once you are in a score-keeping mode, you are stuck in the Us-vs.-Them mode. This does not make for an effective or lasting partnership. Look at each interaction, and always ask yourself if it is fair. If not, then see what you can do to **make** it fair.

You must assure fairness in the setup of your partnering workshop

Forms of Paying

Bid Item

Some owners decide that partnering is going to become a part of their project management policy. They make partnering an option in the bid documents as a bid item, most often as a suggested lump sum amount, an amount that will more than cover the cost of the partnering process. This puts all bidders on an equal footing and ensures that the partnering will be funded if everyone agrees to partnering the project.

Change Order

Upon agreeing that you want to proceed with partnering on your project, you may choose to deal with the associated costs with a change order. Most often the change order issued by the owner to the contractor is for half of the associated partnering costs. The actual contract for the facilitator and the meeting facility is usually with the contractor who is then reimbursed by the owner through the change order. This way of paying allows for flexibility by the owner and the contractor. The bid documents can state the owner's intent to partner, but still allows for the decision to be made once the bid is awarded.

There are many ways to pay for partnering — be creative

Owner Funded

Many owners feel that they have so much at stake with their project that they want to do everything possible to assure success, so they choose to offer partnering on their project and to pay for the associated costs. This is often mentioned in the bid documents, along with a statement of the intention to partner the project.

Contractor Funded

Some contractors, just like some owners, feel that they have a lot at stake, and choose to give their project a better chance for success by partnering. In a public bid situation this may occur when the apparent low bidder is identified. The contractor will approach the owner and suggest partnering, telling the owner that he feels it is so important that he is willing to cover most or all of the associated costs. This usually diffuses the owner's objection that he doesn't have money in the budget for partnering.

Because partnering has proven so successful in reducing claims, some insurance companies will pay for the partnering workshop

Insurance Company/Architect Funded

DPIC (Design Professional Insurance Companies) has been a leader in alternative dispute resolution for its architect and engineer clients for years. It has found partnering to be so successful at managing project risks (and thereby its risks), that the company has designed several programs which will pay for some or all of the associated costs of partnering a project covered under one of its policies. For more information, you may call DPIC at (800) 227-8533.

It is my belief that other contractor-and-owner-focused insurance firms and brokerages also will see the advantages to partnering the projects they insure, so ask your broker if he has a similar program, or would consider one.

Sometimes the simplest solution is the best — split the cost equally

Split Between Parties

Many times the key parties to the project simply decide to partner, and to split the costs equally among themselves. This is a flexible approach, and assures the important buy-in that is necessary for a successful partnering. Responsibilities must be determined, such as who will secure the facilitator, the room, the food, hotel rooms if needed, etc., but this is a good first step toward working together.

EXERCISE:

How will you pay for partnering on your project?

_____

_____

_____

_____

_____

_____

How will you assure that there is buy-in, commitment, and fairness in your funding arrangement?

_____

_____

_____

_____

_____

_____

19
Drafting Partnering Language

Discussion is an exchange of knowledge; argument an exchange of emotion.

Robert Quillen

Drafting Partnering Clauses

Most often it is the owner, architect, or construction manager who develops the language for partnering a project. It is important that your intention or desire to partner is made known, and agreed to by your potential partners. Most often language calling for a "partnering approach" is included in the pre-bid documents, qualification documents, specifications, or contract. It might also be in a letter by the owner, contractor, or architect encouraging the partnering approach. Here are some examples of public agencies' partnering language. I have selected similar agencies so that a comparison of language similarities and differences is more easily made.

It is important that your intention and desire to partner is made known

Caltrans (California Department of Transportation)

PARTNERING - The State will promote the formation of a "Partnering" relationship with the contractor in order to effectively complete the contract to the benefit of both parties. The purpose of this relationship will be to maintain cooperative communication and mutually resolve conflicts at the lowest possible management level.

2

The Contractor may request the formation of such a "Partnering" relationship by submitting a request in writing to the Engineer after approval of the contract. If the Contractor's request for "Partnering" is approved by the Engineer, scheduling of a "Partnering" workshop, selecting the "Partnering" facilitator and workshop site, and other administrative details shall be as agreed to by both parties.

The State will promote the formation of a "Partnering" relationship with the contractor...

3

The costs involved in providing a facilitator and a workshop site will be borne equally by the State and the Contractor. The Contractor shall pay all compensation for the wages and expenses of the facilitator, and of the expenses for obtaining the workshop site. The State's share of such costs will be reimbursed to the Contractor in a change order written by the Engineer. Markups will not be added. All other costs associated with the "Partnering" relationship will be borne separately by the party incurring the costs.

4

The establishment of a "Partnering" relationship will not change or modify the terms and conditions of the contract and will not relieve either party of the legal requirements of the contract.

Pacific Gas and Electric Company

Partnering is the key to success of the Project

Partnering is the key to the success of the Project. PG&E and the contractor will participate in the following meetings.

2.1.1 A partnering retreat will be conducted immediately after Contract award. The location, duration, suggested attendees, and agenda will be developed mutually by both Parties. The purpose of the retreat is to identify and understand common goals, create and foster an environment of trust, and establish partnering objectives and evaluation criteria. Other meetings will plan and coordinate all aspects of the Work so that all requirements are fully understood by both Parties.

2.1.2 Periodic meetings will be held to foster teamwork, review the project status, resolve issues, and to provide performance feedback to both Parties.

Bay Area Rapid Transit District (BART)

SC8.1.1 District Partnering Policy. It is the policy of the District to encourage the Contractor to enter into a "Partnering" arrangement with the District as described below. The Contractor is not obligated to enter into a Partnering arrangement with the District. There will be no penalties of any kind imposed on the Contractor if it elects not to participate in a Partnering arrangement.

Partnering consists of a voluntary effort by ...

Partnering consists of a voluntary effort by the District, the GEC, and the Contractor to develop joint goals and to establish a cooperative atmosphere regarding execution of the construction project. To initiate the Partnering arrangement, the parties will conduct an open discussion prior to the start of the job at a meeting arranged through a Professional Facilitator. It is expected that, at the conclusion of the initial discussion, the parties will express a consensus regarding, among other things, the respective goals in completing the Contract. Thereafter, the parties will continue discussions as necessary and will conduct periodic joint evaluations of performance throughout the life of the Contract. It is expected that the parties will use the services of a Professional Facilitator not only at the initial discussion but, if needed, to assist in later discussions.

SC8.1.2 Partnering Goals. The Goals of Partnering are as follows:

1)   For the Contractor, the GEC, and the District to work as partners;
2)   To avoid confrontation and litigation among the parties;
3)   To reach a mutual understanding on how the construction project is to be conducted; and
4)   To establish an atmosphere of trust and communication.

SC8.1.3 Allowance. An allowance has been included in the Contract to pay the costs of the Professional Facilitator and the expenses of the meeting. The allowance will not cover the salaries and costs of the participants. The Contractor, if it elects to participate in the Partnering arrangement, shall be responsible for payment of the Professional Facilitator and for the meeting expenses and will be reimbursed of these costs from the allowance as described in Section 01025, Measurement and Payment.

> *An allowance has been included in the Contract to pay the costs of the Professional Facilitator and the expenses of the meeting*

SC8.1.4 Contract Rights. The Partnering arrangement will not alter either the District's or the Contractor's legal rights and obligations under the Contract.

Valley Medical Center

P.   PARTNERING AND ALTERNATIVE DISPUTE RESOLUTION:

1.   The County intends to encourage the foundation of a cohesive partnership with the Construction Manager, Contractor, and the Contractor's subcontractors, the County's representative and consultants, and the Architect/Engineer and their consultants. The PARTNERING and Alternative Dispute Resolution Program is detailed in Section 12 of the Project Manual

Arizona Department of Transportation

104.01
(A) Voluntary Partnering:

The Arizona Department of Transportation intends to encourage the foundation of a cohesive partnership with the contractor and its principal subcontractors. This partnership will be structured to draw on the strengths of each organization to identify and achieve reciprocal goals. The objectives are effective and efficient contract performance. Partnering is the key to success of the Project Partnering consists of a voluntary effort by ...An allowance has been included in the Contract to pay the costs of the Professional Facilitator and the expenses of the meeting The County intends to encourage the foundation of a cohesive partnership... and completion within budget, on schedule, and in accordance with plans and Specifications.

> *The County intends to encourage the foundation of a cohesive partnership...*

This partnership will be bilateral in makeup, and participation will be totally voluntary. Any cost associated with effectuating this partnering will be agreed to by both parties and will be shared equally.

To implement this partner initiative within 30 days of notice to award and prior to the preconstruction conference, the contractor's on-site project manager and ADOT's Construction Supervisor will meet and plan a partnering development seminar/team building workshop. At this planning session arrangements will be made to determine attendees at the workshop, agenda of the workshop, duration, and location. Persons required to be in attendance will be the ADOT Construction Supervisor and key project personnel; the contractor's on-site project manager and key project supervision personnel of both the prime and principal subcontractors. The project design engineers and key local government personnel will also be invited to attend as necessary. The contractors and ADOT will also be required to have Regional/District and Corporate/State level managers on the project team.

Follow-up workshops will be held periodically throughout the duration of the contract as agreed by the contractor and Arizona Department of Transportation.

The establishment of a partnership charter on a project will not change the legal relationship of the parties to the contract nor relieve either party from any of the terms of the contract.

The establishment of a partnership charter on a project will not change the legal relationship of the parties...

For negotiated contracts your partnering language might be a letter that states your desire to partner the project. Partnering in the private sector has been going on for several years. As owners seek to limit the number of vendors, they have selected long-term "partners" who make a commitment to working together. The obvious difference between public and private partnering is the ability to choose your partner. In public works there is a statutory requirement for a bid or pre-qualification/low bid selection process involved in selecting the contractor(s). Private projects focus more on developing a long-term relationship. Both lend themselves to developing effective partnerships, but in different ways.

Your partnering language should reflect what you want to accomplish through the partnering process

Your partnering language should reflect what **you** want to achieve through the partnering process. Contracts or specifications can be written so they reward both parties for creating a good partnership.

20

Selecting a Professional Facilitator

Create something out of nothing.

Lao Zi, *The Way of Power*

Selecting a professional facilitator to guide you through the partnering process is an important step. Understanding the role and responsibilities of your facilitator, what qualifications to look for, as well as when and how to bring your facilitator on board, will help you assure success.

A Multi-Discipline Process

Partnering encompasses many different professional disciplines. A partnering facilitator with a background, experience and training in all of these areas is what you are looking for.

Industry Knowledge

Having a background in design and construction is important. A facilitator without this background is not equipped to understand the construction process, industry problems and trends, traditional relationships, and the myriad of processes that surround every project.

While it is important for your facilitator to have a background in the industry, it also is important that they do not come to your project with preconceived ideas on how a project "should" be run. I find that people who have been contractors, architects/engineers, or who worked for owners for many years, are often industry-knowledgeable, but

A partnering facilitator with a background, experience, and training in the many different professional disciplines encompassed by partnering is what you are looking for

that each has specific biases. Look for someone who has industry knowledge, understands the roles of all the players on your project, and has played a different role than the three I mentioned. I have heard of the partnering team actually fighting against the facilitator when the facilitator's opinion of how it "should" be done gets expressed during the pre-partnering or partnering processes.

Facilitation

What makes a good facilitator? Someone who is skilled at drawing people out, allowing the group to explore issues in a creative fashion, and, who, by the end of the session, has empowered the group to pursue its own goals, commitments, and open, honest communication.

In the beginning the facilitator is responsible for setting the climate for the group's interaction. By the end the group should be well-equipped and excited about talking with each other about project issues. So the best facilitator is someone who can exert control to keep the group on track, but allows the group to evolve and develop into an independent unit. Clients tell me horror stories about facilitators who exerted so much control that the participants began to rebel. I also have heard stories about facilitators whose style was so controlling that the participants were not allowed to explore their own issues in the fashion they felt they needed to, but were required to pursue issues chosen by the facilitator.

Good facilitation is an art. It's a balance between control and allowing the group to grow into something new. If this balance is not struck, when the participants leave the workshop, their dependence on the facilitator (who is no longer around) will lead to a rapid erosion of commitment. A skilled facilitator knows when to intervene to keep the group on track and when to stand back and allow the group to evolve.

Training and Training Design

Your facilitator is responsible for designing the process your partnering team will go through. Understanding the process of training and how to design training that meets spe-

A good facilitator is skilled at drawing people out

A good facilitator allows the group to evolve and develop into an independent unit

Good facilitation is an art

cific objectives is an important skill your facilitator must have. The facilitator intervenes only as needed. The facilitator controls the partnering session by designing a process which will lead the group toward its stated objectives.

Your facilitator also should understand that the basic purpose of training is to help build required skills. Many times the facilitator will help the partnering team better understand and deal with the project's issues by teaching the team members new skills which will allow them to deal with those issues more effectively. So your facilitator must be able to identify the skills that are required for a particular group to be effective, or to tackle a particular problem, assess whether or not the group has those skills, and, if not, provide appropriate training to build those skills.

Your facilitator must be able to identify the skills required by a particular group to be successful and then must be able to teach those skills

If your partnering facilitator offers a "cookie-cutter" approach to partnering design, he or she probably doesn't understand the basics of training and training design.

Neutrality/Mediation/Negotiation

Partnering has evolved in the construction and engineering industry out of a desire to eliminate disputes. Partnering is a process for preventing disputes on your project. And, should you have a dispute, it establishes a philosophy for open, honest discussion which often results in early resolution. It is, therefore, important that your facilitator have a background in negotiation and mediation, and understand what it is to act as a neutral party for a group in conflict. Some projects get off to a bad start. It has been my experience that often the partnering team is already in conflict when they come into the partnering session. Your facilitator must understand how to mediate this conflict so that the team can get back on track. Many times there are issues which need to be negotiated, and a skilled facilitator can assist the participants in this negotiation. And, if not at the partnering session, there certainly will be issues that will need to be negotiated at some point in the project.

It is important that your facilitator have a background in negotiation and mediation

The role of a neutral is important to the success of your partnering. As a neutral it is the role of your facilitator to be an objective observer. As such he/she can help move the participants toward the understanding and resolution of their problems, concerns, or conflicts. His/her neutrality is key to being able to make this happen. It also is important that, as a trained neutral, your facilitator will understand how power plays out within the group. A skilled neutral can help "neutralize" power imbalances so that open dialogue can take place.

A facilitator skilled in mediation will be worth their weight in gold when a volatile issue erupts in the session

Sometimes during the partnering session a volatile issue erupts. Your facilitator needs to be skilled in mediation so as to be able to quickly move into a mediative mode and work with the group to resolve the issue. Skilled mediators are not afraid of conflict. They know that conflict can be productive and can be the impetus for creative results which might not otherwise have been possible.

Strategy

The many people and organizations that will work together to design/build your project will come together in your partnering session. During the session, together, you will create the best strategy for working together to complete the project. Strategy encompasses a direction toward which you will head, and the vehicles which will take you there. In your partnering session you will develop a mission statement, which will serve as your direction, and you will develop goals toward meeting your mission, which will serve as your vehicles. It is important that your facilitator understands the power of developing consensus about how to be successful on your project.

A background in strategy planning, strategic thinking, and developing competitive advantage will help you create a good target for your project

A facilitator who has a background in strategy planning, strategic thinking, and developing competitive advantage can help you tremendously in creating a good target (mission) for your project. Strategy gets everyone working together toward a common vision and common goals.

Organizational Development

Many different organizations will come together to work on your project. Each organization brings with it its own culture, norms, rules, regulations, and ways of doing things. This adds to the complexity of communicating, interacting and understanding. A facilitator skilled in organizational development will not be overwhelmed by this diversity and will be able to help the group find common norms and lines of communication, developing a new, mutually agreed upon way of working together. You want a facilitator who understands organizational structures and their potential impact, and who can look at the dynamics of each of the organizations represented. Such a facilitator will have a much greater understanding of the potential conflicts. In partnering you are bringing together people from many different organizations who must find a way to work together effectively, so look for a facilitator who can understand the organizational side of their relationship.

Your facilitator must understand potential organizational conflicts

When to Bring Your Facilitator on Board

As trite as it might sound, the best time to bring your facilitator on board is when you need him. This might be when you discover you need help getting your other project members to understand and agree to partnering. Or, you might need help in writing or designing a partnering process and language for your project. Or, it might be that you need a guide through the process of preparing for your partnering; when you are ready to conduct the pre-partnering process. Bring your facilitator on board when you feel you need help, and the earlier, the better — don't wait until you're in trouble.

The best time to bring your facilitator on board is when you need them

Where to Find a Facilitator

As the popularity of partnering grows so does the number of qualified and experienced partnering facilitators. You'll want to make sure yours is a full-time facilitator, not a moonlighter from some other profession. The best way to find a facilitator for your project is to ask others in the industry who they think is the best. Your trade or professional association often can provide you with a list of names, but usually will not give you advice on who is really good. The International Partnering Institute offers a professional certification program and maintains a list of qualified partnering facilitators (800-805-8300). For more information

Make sure that your facilitator is a full-time facilitator, not a moonlighter from another profession

105

see the Resources section in the back of this book. So ask around. Make sure your facilitator has the background and experience listed above, and talk with a couple of their other clients.

Partnering facilitation is a professional service — would you use a low bid system to select your surgeon?

Partnering facilitation is a professional service. Some organizations use a low-bid system for selecting facilitators. This shows their lack of commitment to partnering and their project. Lowest cost does not equal good service, just as highest cost does not; you need to look at qualifications. However, as with most professions, you get what you pay for. Would you take bids and then go to the cheapest doctor for a medical problem? No, because you would want the best. There is a tiered effect with facilitators. The best are in high demand, and command a higher fee. You have a lot riding on the success of your project, and a lot of money invested. The cost of your professional partnering facilitator will be a small, but significant investment in your project's success. Good enough just doesn't make it; you have too much at stake. Go for the best.

STEP THREE

START THE PRE-PARTNERING PROCESS

21

Understanding Your Partnering Objectives

*We may be very busy, we may be very **efficient**, but we will also be truly **effective** only when we begin with the end in mind.*

Stephen R. Covey
7 Habits of Highly Effective People

Ideally by the time you begin your pre-partnering process you will have your partnering facilitator on board. Your facilitator will help walk you through the pre-partnering process, which will begin by understanding the objectives you and the other key project stakeholders have for partnering.

Every project seeks to be on-time and within budget, but this is a bit broad and general. The clearer and more specific you can be about what you want to accomplish through the partnering process, the better able your facilitator will be to design a process which will lead you there. So to begin you will want to understand some potential objectives. After you think about objectives for your project, I will share the ones I have heard most often during the pre-partnering process.

The clearer and more specific you can be about what you want to accomplish — the better your chances are of succeeding

EXERCISE:

Select a job that you are planning to partner.

Name of job: _____

On the next page list what you hope to accomplish as a result of partnering your project. And specifically what you want to walk away with at the end of the partnering workshop.

Results desired from:
Partnering your project   From the workshop

_____   _____

_____   _____

**The list of
partnering
objectives is best
developed by all
of the key project
members working
together**

_____   _____

_____   _____

_____   _____

_____   _____

_____   _____

This list is best developed by all your key project members working together. This way you will all hear each other's objectives at the same time. So why not invite your future partners over, or have a conference call, and talk about what you want to gain for your project through the partnering process. If such a meeting is not logistically possible, your facilitator can be the conduit for conveying each party's objectives to the other team members. It is important that you only discuss what you might accomplish by partnering and that you not begin the partnering process without the other stakeholders.

*Each project is
unique, yours is,
and so should be
your partnering
objectives*

Partnering Objectives We've Heard along the Way

The following objectives are those I hear most often. Each project and project team is unique, yours is, and so should be your objectives. However, these might help you see if you have covered the bases. It also is important to understand the driving forces for your project. Owners, and contractors, sometimes are driven by forces you wouldn't expect, and these forces shape what they want to achieve. Knowing what they are will help you create the best strategy for assuring that everyone's objectives are met. Those forces might be money, time, quality, public inconvenience, or something else. Find out. It could make the difference between your success and failure.

Improved Working Relationship

Often the owner, contractor, and/or architect/engineer want to improve their working relationship so that they don't slide into what has become the "norm" — an adversarial relationship, which can have an overwhelmingly negative impact on the project. In an adversarial relationship communication is squelched, and you see a lot of "positioning" letters flowing between organizations. Cooperation is a much better approach because, like it or not, you are in this project together — depending upon each other to carry out specific roles and responsibilities. Partnering can go a long way in planting the seeds of a good working relationship.

Improved working relationships is the most often mentioned objective for a partnering

Part of developing an improved working relationship can include getting to know each other, or know each other better, understanding project roles and responsibilities, understanding each other's expectations, developing and improving lines of communication, and building trust. The more specific you can be about what an improved working relationship would be like, the better chance you have for developing one.

Reduce the Risk of Disputes/Litigation

The next most often heard objective for partnering is to reduce the risk of unresolved disputes or the potential for litigation. Partnering opens up communication among the project team members. There evolves an agreed-upon expectation that problems will be discussed in an open and honest fashion and worked out together. Being willing to work through issues before they become serious problems, and mutually creating potential solutions, will go a long way toward preventing disputes. A related objective might be to understand alternative dispute-resolution processes and develop such a process. You will want your process to

Being willing to work through issues before they become serious problems goes a long way toward preventing disputes

resolve disputes quickly and at the lowest level possible. Above all, most project teams have the objective to stay out of court.

Reduce the Risk of Slowdowns

Time is money, so every slowdown is a threat to the success of your project. Partnering can help by improving the understanding of the project schedule, the purpose and use of the schedule, the form of the schedule, and what needs and needs not to be included on the schedule. Far too often a schedule is seen as an instrument of enforcement rather than as a tool for managing the project, so miscommunication about the schedule is rampant. Gaining agreement on the use of the schedule(s) can go a long way. You might also add to the schedule items from your partnering that you have agreed are important to monitor.

Far too often a schedule is seen as an instrument of enforcement, rather than as a tool for managing the project

Slowdowns also occur when decisions don't get made in a timely fashion. This can occur for many reasons, but most often it is due to a lack of understanding of the decision making-process within your or others' organizations. Developing agreed-upon interorganizational processes can help. Partnering can ensure that you have a champion for your issues within the organization where the decision is to be made.

Changes happen. They can raise havoc with your schedule. Partnering can help to develop a process for dealing effectively with changes so they have less impact on your project. You can work to develop a proactive problem-solving process and mind-set that swings into action when a change occurs.

Changes happen

Increase Productivity

Every project team member would like to do more in less time, and maintain quality, of course. This is the basis of productivity improvement. Partnering can assist by developing and building upon common interests, so you have a committed crew and project team, all heading in the same direction. You can work to manage any conflicting interests among the various stakeholders, so you work together, not against each other. You can coordinate delivery of materials, improve staging, and assure testing, staking, and other services happen in a timely fashion. You also have the opportunity in your partnering workshop to unleash the years of experience and expertise of your team. This can result in finding creative ways to approach the project and its problems.

Tackle a Tough Technical Issue

Partnering can help you identify tough technical issues up front, so you can work together to tackle them. This proactive approach significantly increases your odds for success. After understanding the intent and need of the designer and owner, the team can then work together to agree on an approach to the issues that is acceptable to all.

You have years, sometimes decades or even centuries, of experience in your partnering session — take advantage of it

Often disputes which have ended up in litigation are couched in technical terms but are the result of a breakdown in communication, and thus are relationship problems, explaining why a solution was not found. Partnering can assist in such a situation.

Improve the Overall Project

Partnering was born out of the quality movement. Improving quality entails working toward innovation, doing things in new and better ways. Partnering offers the potential for innovation on your project. Resources or time might be tight and you may be seeking help in saving money or improving the schedule. Your project might be difficult and complex, with many challenges, and you may be seeking ways to make it easier. You will know to whom you should talk about which issue as you get to know each other. Partnering can, overall, help ensure your project's success.

Improving quality entails doing things in new and better ways — partnering offers the potential for innovation on your project

22

The Pre-Partnering Process

The proprietor or manager must also be willing to listen... That attitude is a necessary part of successful management based on the collective wisdom of the firm.

Konoshke Matsushita
Not for Bread Alone

The pre-partnering process is conducted by your facilitator. This is how the facilitator obtains information and gains an understanding about the nature of the project, the existing relationships, the challenges that you see. It also is where you share your objectives for the partnering and the partnering workshop that you identified from the exercise in chapter 21.

Gaining an Understanding

Information is gathered from each of the key project stakeholders. The purpose of the pre-partnering process is to help the facilitator gain an understanding of the current status of the project and the expectations of the participants, to find out what each participant wishes to gain from the partnering effort, and to assess the skills and/or processes that might be required to get there.

Armed with all of this information your facilitator will begin the design process. Designing always starts with the end in mind. The facilitator will back up from the end point to determine the necessary steps to getting there. This can be a real challenge when one or two project stakeholders have opposite objectives. When this occurs, the facilitator can help the stakeholders see that there is a misalignment of expectations. Together everyone can work to agree on what can and will be achieved through the partnering process.

Armed with an understanding of the current status of the project and the expectations of the participants, your facilitator begins the design process

Methods of Pre-Partnering

There are several methods that have proven effective for pre-partnering. Your facilitator should choose the one that best meets the needs of your project and that is possible. For example, it usually is best to meet and talk with each participant, but logistics and timing often make this impossible. It is important that you support the facilitator's efforts to gain the information and understanding required to design the best possible partnering workshop process. Your facilitator may select one or more of the following methods.

Face-to-face Meeting
There is nothing as effective as being able to meet with the project stakeholders face-to-face to discuss the project, their opinions, experience, objectives and concerns. Depending on the nature of the project and the project problems, your facilitator might decide to meet with individuals, meet with each organization, or meet with the whole project team. Each meeting serves a specific purpose.

With individual meetings the facilitator gains a clear insight into each person's vantage point. The facilitator will see where there are built-in conflicts.

Meeting with each organization gives the facilitator insight into what the organization sees are the issues, concerns and expectations. This often can be revealing to the individuals in the organization because often they do not share the same expectations at the beginning of the meeting. This serves to get the members of the organization "on the same page" before they meet with the other partnering team members.

Meeting with the whole project team, with each organization being represented, offers an opportunity for everyone to share expectations and gain an understanding, and agreement, of what they want to walk away with as a result of the partnering. With this understanding participants are already moving toward an agreed-upon outcome when they begin the partnering workshop.

There are several methods for conducting the pre-partnering — your facilitator will select the one best suited for your project

Meeting with each organization gives the facilitator insight into each organization's issues, concerns, and expectations

Individual Phone Interview

Conducting interviews with key individuals by phone is another effective way for the facilitator to gain insight and understanding. By asking questions the facilitator will obtain insights similar to those she would get from a face-to-face interview, but some information will be lost without the dimension of body language.

Conference Call

A group meeting by phone (conference call) gives the facilitator the ability to bring everyone together to discuss objectives, concerns, and desires in a forum where everyone can hear, discuss and agree. If too many people are on the call, it can become difficult to know who is talking, and the time required to allow for each participant to speak may make the call cumbersome. I have found that a conference call with two to five people works remarkably well. The obvious advantage of a conference call is that the participants don't need to be in the same room, the same city, or even the same country.

> *A well planned phone interview is a good substitute for a face-to-face meeting*

Questionnaire

A pre-partnering questionnaire helps give the facilitator some routine information as well as jogging the minds of those completing it. Some clients like the questionnaire better than an interview because they have a chance to think about their answers and it is less intrusive on their time. Questionnaires can be sent to a wide range of people, offering the facilitator a broad scope of feedback. The questionnaire can be sent and responded to electronically, by e-mail or fax, making it a fast process.

Following is example pre-partnering questionnaire. It gives the facilitator a basic understanding of the project.

> *Some clients like a questionnaire better than an interview — it gives them more time to think about their answers*

I can't express strongly enough how critical the pre-partnering process is to the success of your partnership. This is where the facilitator begins to understand the lay of the land, and begins to develop a road map to get you to where you want to go.

ORGMETRICS

Pre-Partnering Questionnaire

Congratulations on your decision to partner this project. Partnering is a proven way to reduce conflict and manage risk while increasing project productivity

Project	
Organization	
To	
Session Date	
Please return by	FAX (510) 449-0945

It is our experience that each partnering is unique. The people, the project, the location, the history of the project, and its team make each session different. We try to design each session to meet the outcomes that you want. Taking a few minutes to complete this questionnaire will greatly assist us in designing your partnering session.

As time is of the essence, please return the completed questionnaire as soon as possible. Hopefully, we will also have an opportunity to discuss your answers so that I can have a complete understanding of the project and your expectations. Thank you for your help in making this a great session.

PROJECT OVERVIEW	
Project Name	
Project Type	
Project Duration	
Contract Value	
Owner	
Designer	
Other Key Agencies	
Construction to Start	
Project Complexity Description	
How Complex is this project?	
Where are the challenges?	

Pre-partnering should be included in the facilitation fee you pay unless your project requires an extensive amount of investigation in order to understand the issues and needs before the design process can begin. In that case, it is normal for there to be an additional fee to cover the extra work.

PROJECT OVERVIEW	
Number of Subcontractors	
General information regarding the nature of this project	
Please describe this projectchallenges?	

Partnering Session Objectives - What do you want to walk away with as a result of our partnering session?

1. _____   4. _____
   _____   _____

2. _____   5. _____
   _____   _____

3. _____   6. _____
   _____   _____

Potential Project Issues - What do you see as potential project issues or challenges?

_____   _____

_____   _____

Partnering Potential

                 low   high

1) What is your level of commitment to this partnership? 1   2   3   4   5

2) What might be roadblocks to effectively partnering this project?

_____

_____

_____

_____

_____

Figure 16

119

Who needs to attend?

It is important to include those who are key to the success of the project. Besides your key project team, this also may include the designer, funding agency, effected agencies or cities, key subs and suppliers, or anyone who can impact the project and needs to understand and buy into the project's mission and goals. For best results, one-day sessions should be limited to fifteen to twenty people. Two-day sessions should be limited to fifteen to thirty people.

Estimated number of participants:

On a separate piece of paper, please type a joint list of all attendees, including each person's name, title, and organization.

Partnering Session Groups

The partnering session will be most effective if those who will be working together during the project are together in the same group.

Place those attendees who will be working together, or who need to work together, on this project into the same group. Groups work best if they are comprised of five to eight people. Please indicate on your list of attendees which group each person should be assigned to by writing a group number next to each name. Final group assignments will be made by the facilitator.

PARTNERING LOGISTICS	
Session location	
Meeting planner	Phone

Finally, we need a copy of each of the main company/agency's logo to incorporate into the partnering workbook. Usually sending us an original piece of letterhead works fine.

23

Looking for a Custom-Designed Workshop

Insight allows you to see beyond the present

Mark McCormack

What They Don't Teach You at Harvard Business School

Designing a partnering workshop and process that will help make your project the best it can be is usually a lot of work. It requires specialized skills, as discussed in chapter 20. It takes time, sometimes a lot of time, to create new exercises and activities. For these reasons many facilitators have chosen a "cookie-cutter" approach to partnering, rather than custom designing the process for each project.

It takes time and specialized skills to design a custom workshop

This "cookie-cutter" approach can have disastrous results for your project. The partnering workshop should be designed to meet the specific needs of your project and your project partners, as we discussed in chapter 22. The partnering workshop serves as the road map to your desired destination. If you are in San Francisco and you want to go over the Golden Gate Bridge, it would be difficult to find the best path if you only had a road map of Chicago. This is what a "cookie-cutter" partnering workshop can mean to your project; that you never get on the best path possible for success.

Many facilitators use a "cookie-cutter" approach to partnering — often with disastrous results

What you should be looking for is a workshop that has been specifically developed to meet the expressed objectives of the various project team members.

How to Spot a Custom-Designed Workshop

First you will know that the facilitator has talked or met with the key project team members. Ask her how she will go about custom-designing a workshop. A partnering facilitator who has been around for awhile will have many different "modules" available for use in your session. Ask about them and the potential outcomes from their use. Ask if the facilitator is going to develop something specific for your workshop. A workbook should be created for each session that reflects the session's unique design. Ask to see sample workbooks from other partnering sessions conducted by the facilitator. Chapter 26 contains an example of the skeleton of a typical partnering workshop. The customized modules used for your workshop probably will fit into this skeleton. However, your project and its issues might be so unique that it needs something entirely new. Ask if the facilitator sees such a need for your project. You want to have confidence that your facilitator understands all of your objectives for partnering and is planning to lead your partnering team toward accomplishing those objectives.

An experienced facilitator will have many different "modules" available for use in your partnering session

Customizing entails not only the design of your workshop, but also the flexibility to change in midstream. You want to make sure that your facilitator has the experience and expertise to be flexible during the workshop should things take an unpredicted path. Ask the facilitator how he would handle a significant change of direction during the workshop.

Customization also means being able to make changes in midstream during the workshop

Other Design Factors

Deciding Who Needs To Attend
Deciding who needs to attend the workshop to gain consensus and understanding among all the important project stakeholders is an important design element. The facilitator will ask you who you think needs to attend given the specific objectives you have stated. Use the rule-of-thumb that if you are in doubt if someone should be included, it often is best to include them. The size of your partnering team also may determine how many can effectively attend, and

thus who can attend. The optimal size of the partnering workshop is fifteen to twenty-five people. I have conducted workshops with five people and with as many as sixty-five. With too few people, the workshop lacks the kind of feedback that stimulates the mind and leads discussion into new dimensions of thinking. With too many, it is difficult for the participants to get to know each other, understand their roles and responsibilities, and have enough time to share ideas and concerns. There is a point of diminishing return in the number of people who attend, so you want the *key* project stakeholders, those who are most concerned with its success, or those who can have a strong impact on the project, especially given your objectives.

Just like Goldilocks, you want the number of participants in your partnering session to be "just right"

For example, one project team decided during its partnering session to accelerate the schedule. The project had many outside regulatory agencies who had to "buy-into" to this new schedule. Unfortunately, the regulators had not been invited to the partnering session. As a result, the project had many problems with a couple of the regulators, requiring another partnering that included them. Including the regulators made all the difference to the success of the project, which was completed significantly ahead of schedule.

Grouping Attendees

Since in a one-, two-, or even three-day partnering session it is difficult to get to know twenty to thirty people well, it is important to break into smaller work groups. These groups usually stay together throughout the partnering workshop. The selection of who will be in which group, therefore, should be part of your session's design. One of the first decisions your facilitator will make is whether to have homogeneous or mixed groups. To make the decision the facilitator might ask questions similar to these:

Deciding how to group the participants requires experience and insight — but the results are worth the effort

- Who needs to interface with whom during the project?
- Is there an important issue around which we need to group people?
- Do we have a variety of organizations with divergent opinions so that we need to put one representative from each organization in each group?

Your assistance will greatly help the facilitator make the right decisions in selecting the groupings. These groupings have a dramatic impact on the outcome of your session, so give the facilitator the information she needs to help her understand who each person is and what their perspective might be.

It's important that you identify the participants to the facilitator as soon as possible

The importance of your small groups makes it important that you identify who will attend and inform the facilitator as soon as possible. Your facilitator might ask you further questions after the pre-partnering process to make sure you have the right people, and may suggest the addition or deletion of certain people.

Meeting Place, Room Setup and Atmosphere

Where you hold you partnering workshop is also a part of its design. The meeting place should be clean, warm, comfortable, have electricity, and be well lighted. I have held sessions in rooms where there were no wall plugs for a computer or overhead projector, no heat, no air conditioning, where it was so dark you could not read your own name, and where trains came by every few minutes making so much noise that the session had to stop. All of these distractions can impair the success of your session.

The meeting place should be at a neutral location — not the world headquarters of one of the participants

Besides being comfortable, your meeting place should be at a neutral location, and agreed upon by all the key stakeholders. What constitutes a neutral location will vary greatly among different groups. Some might want to go to a training room located in a different building within their agency; others might want to go downtown to a local hotel or conference center. Either way, the attendees must agree that the chosen location is an appropriate site for your workshop. Ask your facilitator for a recommendation.

Another aspect in the selection of the meeting place is whether people will spend the night, eat meals together, and/or have an opportunity to socialize. Your workshop can be a retreat where people get away from their daily routine to focus in on the project and get to know one another. Or, it can be a workday session, where everyone arrives just in time for the start and leaves as soon as the session concludes. With a workday session there is little opportunity for social interaction, and unless controlled there can be many interruptions from pagers, cellular phones, or people leaving just to "check-in" with their offices.

Cost and attendees' time usually are the determining factors, but the above are real considerations if you want your partnering to have the best chance possible for being nurtured along, especially during the critical first days.

Interruptions must be controlled — no pagers, cellular phones or individual breaks to "check-in" with the office

24

Deciding the Workshop's Length

A company, or any group for that matter, composed of people who know themselves and who can deal adequately with any given situation will be successful.

Konosuke Matsushi
Founder, Matsushi Electric Industrial Company, Ltd.

A two-day partnering workshop has become the norm. However, you may decide on a one-day or multiple-day session given the nature of your project and the issues you face. In this chapter we will look at each of these sessions and determine which is the best match for your project.

Being Needs-Driven

The length of your partnering workshop should be based on the needs of the project and project team, not on convenience. Far too often the decision is based on the notion that "we don't want to spend the time" rather than on what will give the best return on your investment of time, money and commitment. Spending too little time can seriously decrease your partnership's potential, as can spending too much time. Determining the appropriate amount of time to achieve the desired objectives of the partnering must be the major focus.

Don't base the length of your partnering workshop on convenience

Time Impacts

Certain elements of the partnering impact the need for time. These include the size of the group, the number of problems or issues, and the number of organizations which are represented. Each of these increases the need for time in your session.

Certain elements of the partnering impact the need for time

EXERCISE:

To help you determine the required time for your partnering workshop, you can rate each of the potential time/needs impacts as they relate to your project.

TIMES/NEEDS IMPACT		Score
Number of Attendees	for 10-15 score 1 for 20-30 score 2 for more than 30 score 3	
Number of Key Organizations	for 3 or less score 1 for 4-6 score 2 for more than 6 score 3	
Size of project	if small score 1 if medium score 2 if large score 3	
Complexity of Project	if not complex score 1 if complex score 2 if very complex score 3	
Difficulty of Project	if routine-to-challenging score 1 if difficult score 2 if very difficult score 3	
Relationships/Reputations	if good score 1 if unknown-to-poor score 2 if poor-to-bad score 3	

Score:

Low scores (1s) indicate a one-day session is appropriate, middle scores (2s) indicate that a two-day session is appropriate, and high scores (3s) indicate that a multiple-day or other series of sessions is appropriate. Where does you project fall: do you have more 1s, 2s, or 3s?

Let Your Facilitator Help

Your professional partnering facilitator, if you have selected one based on the guidelines in chapter 20, will work on fifty to one hundred different projects each year. She can be a great resource for how long your partnering session needs to be. Let her help you. Most people make the mistake of deciding how long their workshop will be before the facilitator has done any of the pre-partnering. The decision should be made based on the results of the pre-partnering. Before that, it really is impossible to know the exact needs for the workshop. Talk with your facilitator after he has completed the pre-partnering process and then make the decision.

Funding also often drives the decision. Sometimes a decision must be made so that it can be included in the bid documents. If this is the case, use the exercise in this chapter at the time you prepare the bid documents to make your best estimate of what type of workshop will be needed. Further guidance to assist you in making a decision follows.

The length of the partnering session will be determined from the results of the pre-partnering process

When To Use A One-Day Session

Let me start by saying that you can accomplish a lot in one day. What you lose in a one-day session compared to a two-day session is the time to do some real team building and relationship development. People just don't move that fast to be open and develop trust. But, in one day you can get through all of the component parts of developing your partnership. As demonstrated in this chapter's exercise, one-day sessions are best for smaller, uncomplicated projects that have fewer organizations involved. By small I mean small for the team members. For example, if you have never done a $1 million job before, then for you that is a large job. If you routinely do $25 million jobs, then it would be a small job for you. Remember to consider the other team members. What might be small for one team member could be large for another. Talk to each other. Complexity increases with size. A $25 million job is going to be more complex than a $1 million job. One-day sessions are sometimes used as a kick-off, with a follow-up workshop scheduled within three to four months after construction starts.

A lot can be accomplished in one day — especially on smaller, less complicated projects

Sample One-Day Partnering Session Agenda

7:30	Continental Breakfast
8:00	Opening Statements
	Project's History
	Introductions
	Expectations/Rules
	Partnering Overview
	Team Building/Skill Building Activity
	The Power of Paradigms
	Vision/Mission Statement
	IPOs (Issues, Problems/Barriers, Opportunities)
	Key Issues for Success
12:00	Lunch
	Creative Problem Solving/Goal Setting for Key Issues
	Development of a Dispute Resolution Process
	Evaluation Process
	Making Partnering Real
	Signing of the Partnering Agreement
4:00	End of Session

Figure 17

Two-day sessions are optimal for most projects, but with a skilled facilitator a lot can be accomplished in one day

When to Use a Two-Day Session

In two days you have time to develop relationships and trust

Two-day sessions are optimal for most projects. In two days you have time to develop relationships and trust, demonstrate you commitment to partnering and to the project, and explore potential problem areas. As the size and complexity of the project increases you will need more time. When more organizations are represented, this, too, means more time will be required. One project I am working on has seven different owner organizations and twenty different design firms. This project can't possibly be approached in the same way as a project with one owner and one designer. Two-day sessions also are best when there may be some issues already erupting. The extra time can help you get your project back on track, by working together to solve those issues.

Sample Two-Day Partnering Session Agenda

Day 1		Day 2	
7:30	Continental Breakfast	7:30	Continental Breakfast

8:00	Opening Statements
	    Introductions
	    Expectations/Rule
	    Partnering Overview
		8:00	Recap of Day One

			Homework Assignment
			    Sharing of Most Valuable Experiences
			    Sharing of Job Requirements

	Team Building Activity		
	The Design/Build Game	ties)	IPOs (Issues, Problems/Barriers, Opportuni-
12:00	Lunch		Key Issues (1-3)

	Design/Build Game (continued)		Creative Problem Solving for Key Issues
			    Problem Finding
			    Fact Finding
			    Solution Finding
			    Goal Setting and Action Planning

	Exploring Interests		
	Paradigms		
	Vision/Mission		
	Homework Assignment	12:00	Lunch
	My Job Requirements and Most Valuable Experience		Creative Problem Solving (continued)
4:30	End of Day One		Development of a Dispute Resolution Process
6:30	Group Dinner		Development of an Evaluation Process
			Signing of the Partnering Agreement
		4:00	End of Session

Figure 18

When to Use a Multiple-Day Session

Multiple-day sessions give you time for some real skill-building, team-building and problem-solving. Or, if you have many players and organizations, more than two days may be required to form your partnership. Most often these are consecutive days, but sometimes they are not. You might not be able to get your team to commit to three or four days away from their work, but you can get them to commit to two two-day sessions two weeks apart. In the multiple-day session you have time to really gain buy-in and to look for ways to improve your project. I have seen split multiple-day sessions work best when some skills were taught to the whole group, then practiced throughout the rest of the session, and in the interim until the next two-day session, and then reinforced at that session. Large, complex projects or ones where relationships have deteriorated are best dealt with in this fashion. Advanced partnering methods are discussed in chapter 39.

Multi-day sessions do not necessarily have to be on consecutive days

25
Planning the Meeting

It is better to be prepared for an opportunity and not have one than to have an opportunity and not be prepared.

Whitney Young, Jr.

Designating a Meeting Planner

As soon as you have agreed to partner your project, a meeting planner should be designated. This person will be in charge of making all of the meeting arrangements for your workshop. As described in chapter 18, this job can be an important way to gain a commitment to the partnership, especially if only one participant is paying for the entire workshop. If the costs are being split, then either party can serve as the meeting planner; many times it is not someone who will attend the session.

You should reserve a meeting room as soon as the date for the partnering is agreed upon

Selecting a Facility

As soon as the date for your partnering session has been set, you should immediately secure a meeting site. Meeting rooms are available at hotels, restaurants, conference centers, and sometimes community centers. The workshop can be held at any appropriate facility. It is best if the session is held at a neutral site, away from day-to-day interruptions. There should be ample light, and heat or air conditioning available for comfort. Because this is a working session, it will require more space than a hotel would normally allow for the number of participants: approximately 1,000 square feet for every ten to twenty-five attendees. (Refer to Chapter 23 to review how your meeting place can affect the outcome of your session.)

Because this is a working session, it will require more space than a hotel would normally allow for the number or participants

The Chamber of Commerce or Visitors Bureau in the area where the meeting is to be held can assist you in finding potential facilities. The American Automobile Association publishes directories for almost every city in the country that can be helpful in seeing what might be available in a specific area. They are provided free to AAA members. For reservations at hotels, restaurants or conference centers you will probably work through their catering departments.

You can expect to pay a room rental fee between $100 and $350 per day

You can expect to pay a room rental fee at most hotels, conference centers and some restaurants. This usually runs $100 to $350 per day. It is sometimes possible to have the fee waived if you mention that you are not accustomed to paying a fee when you are being served a meal in the room. Flexibility of fees is usually a matter of hotel occupancy rates; if the hotel is busy and in demand you probably will have to pay some amount, but negotiate and you may be able to drastically reduce the fee.

You should send a notice of the meeting to each of the attendees, or, at a minimum, their organizations

Inviting the Participants

You should send a "notice of meeting" or invitation to each of the attendees (or organizations) two to four weeks in advance of the partnering session. This notice should include a request for confirmation of their attendance, the date, time, and location of the workshop, along with directions to the facility, and other important information, such as the hotel's reservations number for those who wish to stay overnight. Ask your participants to respond within seven days to confirm their attendance by submitting a list of attendees with their titles and roles in the project. This list should be forwarded to the facilitator as soon as it is available (at least one week prior to the session).

Here is a sample letter of invitation.

Date

Sam the Man, Resident Engineer
Department of Transportation
Great Highway Street
Somewhere, America

Subject: Confirmation of our Partnering Workshop for
           Important Bridge Project

Dear Sam:

You and your project team are cordially invited to attend a partnering workshop between our respective organizations for the Important Bridge Project. I am excited about working together to make this a great project. As we have already agreed, the session will take place as follows:

Date: February 14 & 15, 2005
Time: 7:30 A.M. - 5:00 P.M.
Place: Thataway Conference Center (a map is enclosed)
          1200 Thataway Road
          Roadrunner, America
          (800) XXX-XXXX

Rooms: A block of rooms has been secured at a special rate. Please call the hotel directly to make your room reservation.

Please confirm and forward to me by [date] the names and titles of all your project team members who will be attending our session. We can then work with the facilitator to assure the seating arrangements. You can reach me at XXX-XXXX if you have any questions, or if I can help in any way.

Sincerely,

Good-Guy Contractor

Figure 19

Selecting Refreshments and Meals

Most partnering sessions begin with a continental breakfast approximately half an hour before the session starts

You will work with the catering department to select a menu for the session. Most partnering sessions begin with a continental breakfast approximately half an hour before the session starts. This is an important time for the participants to begin to socialize and get to know one another. Coffee is usually refreshed at 10:00 A.M. Lunch is served (ideally in a room outside the meeting room so there is less disruption to the session) at 12:00 noon. Refreshments of soda, iced tea and cookies are usually served at 2:00 P.M. Many times, either the evening prior to the workshop or the first evening of the workshop, the team will have a group dinner. Menus will have to be selected for each of these meals. The catering department will provide you with its menu and price list from which you can select. It is important that you tell the catering department that you have only thirty to forty-five minutes for lunch. This will help to assure speed in delivery and service. You cannot take a one-and-a-half to two hour lunch and get through the workshop process. Be careful of buffet lunches where you make your own sandwich as it can take an hour for all the participants just to get through the line.

The room setup is part of the design of the workshop

Assuring the Correct Room Setup

The room setup is part of the design of the workshop. Your facilitator probably will advise you of what is needed. How the room is set up is an important consideration in the design of your workshop, so make sure you understand what is required. Your facilitator may provide you with a schematic for your session which can be sent to the catering department. Here are a couple of examples.

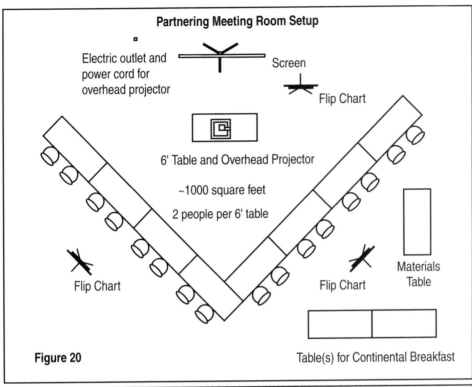

Partnering Meeting Room Setup

Electric outlet and power cord for overhead projector

Screen

Flip Chart

6' Table and Overhead Projector

~1000 square feet

2 people per 6' table

Flip Chart

Flip Chart

Materials Table

Figure 20

Table(s) for Continental Breakfast

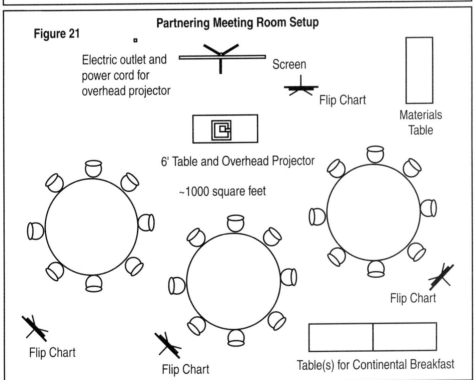

Partnering Meeting Room Setup

Figure 21

Electric outlet and power cord for overhead projector

Screen

Flip Chart

Materials Table

6' Table and Overhead Projector

~1000 square feet

Flip Chart

Flip Chart

Flip Chart

Table(s) for Continental Breakfast

Audio-Visual Requirements

Your facilitator should provide you with a list of audio-visual needs. This probably will include a flip chart for each group, and one for the facilitator, an overhead projector and screen, and possibly a VCR and TV or slide projector. These can be secured through the catering department and probably will be charged to the meeting room's bill. If your facility does not have these available, you often can rent them from an audio-visual rental firm. It is important that all the audio-visual equipment be in place at least an hour prior to the partnering team's arrival. This will allow the facilitator to finalize setting up the session and still have time to greet participants as they arrive.

Audio Visual equipment can usually be obtained through the catering department

Overnight Accommodations

For some sessions overnight accommodations will be required for some or all of the participants. You can book a block of rooms in the name of your group, usually at a specially negotiated lower-than-normal rate. This is done through the facility's sales department. These rooms will be held for you until a specified date, after which any not reserved will be released. If a government entity is one of the parties in your partnering, special government rates may be available to you. If you do book a block of rooms you should let your participants know the room rate, and the deadline for making their reservations. You are not responsible for paying for the rooms in your block unless you specifically tell the sales department that you wish to do so.

Book a block of rooms in the name of your group for those requiring overnight stays

Paying the Bill

If there is time, you can request that a corporate account be set up, and at the conclusion of the session you will be billed. Or, the meeting planner may designate someone to pay by credit card or check upon the workshop's conclusion. It is important that the bill be reviewed for accuracy.

Meeting Planning Check List

❏ Date Selected

❏ Facility Selected

❏ Invitations sent to participants notifying them of session location and time

❏ Corporate account set up or arrangements made to pay by credit card or check

❏ Room schematic sent to facility's meeting coordinator

❏ Arrangement agreed to by facility

❏ Minimum 1,000 square feet per ten to twenty-five participants (2,500 square feet for twenty-five to thirty-five)

❏ Electrical outlets/extension cord available for computer and overhead projector (and VCR, if required)

❏ Continental breakfast ordered

❏ Coffee service at 10:00 A.M. ordered

❏ Lunch arrangements made

❏ Snack service at 2:00 P.M. ordered

❏ Overhead projector and screen obtained

❏ Flip charts and easels (one per group plus one for the facilitator) obtained

❏ Other audio-video equipment needs secured (i.e. VCR/TV, slide projector)

❏ Rooms blocked for overnight participants

❏ List of attendees forwarded to facilitator

❏ Group dinner arranged

Figure 22

STEP FOUR

HOLD YOUR PARTNERING SESSION

26

The Partnering Skeleton

Don't wish it were easier, wish you were better.

Jim Rohn

You are now ready to hold your partnering session. Step 4 will give you an idea of what your session might be like. Although each partnering session is unique to the project and its team members, there is a core of components that should be in most partnering sessions. The partnering skeleton illustrates these components.

Partnering Session Skeleton

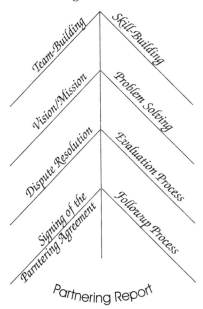

> Even though every partnering session is unique, each has a basic set of components at the core

Figure 23

These partnering components may be sequenced differently from the order shown to best meet the needs of your project. However, each component should be included in some fashion. These components are designed to build consensus within the project team, and co-create project objectives. Remember that, in essence, together you are developing a strategic plan for your project.

The basic partnering session components might appear in a different order from project to project — but they all must be present

Team-building, skill-building, vision, mission, problem-solving, dispute resolution, and signing of the partnering agreement will be covered in detail in the Step 4 chapters. Step 5 chapters will detail an evaluation process, a follow-up process, and describe your partnering report. Briefly, here is a summation of each of these chapters.

Team-Building

You will enter the room probably not knowing some or many of the other participants. It is important that you get to know each other. It also is important that you begin to act and think as a team. This chapter will discuss activities which will lead toward these objectives.

Skill-Building

It may be necessary for the partnering team to learn a new skill that will directly improve the team's ability to solve project problems

Before we start discussing the specifics of the project, it may be necessary that the partnering team learn a new skill or two which will directly benefit the team's ability to solve its project problems. Some training and practice with the new skill(s), before introducing real project problems, can go a long way to assuring the success of solving real problems. Example skills include active listening, understanding social styles, negotiation, etc.

Vision/Mission

Having a target to aim at gives the team a touchstone for the entire project. Your vision of what would make this an ideal project, and a mission statement specifying what you are committing to accomplish together, gives the team direction and purpose.

Problem-Solving

Working together to solve current or potential project problems gives the team practice at coming to agreement and working through diverse issues. It also is a chance to practice solving problems before they impact the project, as well as an opportunity to better understand each team member's point of view, hidden strengths and expectations.

Dispute Resolution

Partnering for the most part is an improved framework for communication that helps prevent disputes. The team will develop an agreed-upon dispute resolution process, so that if a dispute arises there is a process which the team can follow to resolve it. Thus disputes will be solved quickly and not allowed to fester and erode relationships.

> *Partnering, for the most part, is an improved framework for communication that helps prevent disputes*

Evaluation Process

What gets measured gets done. It is important to measure progress toward achieving your mission and the condition of your partnering relationship. You will need to discuss new issues as they arise as well as measure how you are doing with the commitments you already have made. The team will develop a process for measuring this progress.

Follow-Up Process

It may be important to the success of the partnership that the partnering team meet again, and re-commit to one another, especially since many projects span one, two, or more years. The commitments made at your partnering session must be revisited, and changed as appropriate, so that the team can remain committed. Far too often teams fail to check in with each other and re-commit to their partnership until things start to unravel. It is far easier to accomplish re-commitment when things are still going well.

> *What gets measured gets done*

Signing the Partnering Agreement

Your Partnering Agreement (or Partnering Charter as it also is called) will be signed at the end of your partnering workshop. When you sign this agreement you are pledging your personal commitment to working toward accomplishing the mission and goals, abiding by the dispute resolution and evaluation processes, and keeping any other commitments that have been made. This is NOT a legal document, but rather a personal commitment among the team members.

Your Partnering Report

After your partnering session is over, your partnering facilitator will create a partnering report which includes all of the information you created during your session. This includes vision, mission, goals, action plans, processes, etc. The report will be sent to the meeting planner (or other designated persons) for distribution to the partnering team members. The report stands as a record and reminder of what has been committed to, and what you are aiming to accomplish on your project.

When you sign the partnering agreement you are pledging your personal commitment to working toward accomplishing the project's mission and goals

27
Building a Team

Groups become teams through disciplined action. They shape a common purpose, agree on performance goals, define a common working approach, develop high levels of complementary skills, and hold themselves mutually accountable for results.

Jon R. Katzenbach and Douglas K. Smith
The Wisdom of Teams

Forging a team from a group of individuals and several different organizations who have come together to build your project is the first phase in your partnering session. This process can be divided into four parts: breaking the ice; getting to know each other; gaining understanding; and beginning to act like a team. I also will share with you some examples of team-building exercises which have proven to be successful.

DILBERT reprinted by permission of United Feature Syndicate, Inc.

Figure 24

Team building can be divided into four parts: ice breaking; getting to know each other; understanding; and beginning to act as a team

Breaking the Ice

Informal Social Time
Your partnering workshop probably will begin with a group dinner the evening before the first day's session, or a continental breakfast just before the session starts. This time is important as people begin to meet and greet each other informally, beginning to break down the barriers between them.

Welcome and Setting the Stage

As we discussed in chapter 15, upper management must be committed to your partnering. This commitment can be demonstrated by a representative from senior management making some opening remarks at the beginning of the session, setting the stage for the partnering process. In some organizations the project team will not openly share without upper management's permission.

Project Vision and Overview

We often make the assumption that we know what the project is and what we are supposed to do. It has been my experience that this knowledge is different for each person in the partnering session. If I'm the electrical contractor I see the project as the electrical systems I must construct. If I'm the utility contractor I see it as the underground improvements I must make. Many times, the construction team does not have a good appreciation for the overall project and what it means to the owner and the project's future users. Having a presentation of the vision for the project can help enormously toward bonding everyone together for this important project. Since a picture is worth a thousand words, slides, architectural renderings, photographs or models all help to make the project vision real.

Many times the construction team does not have a good appreciation for the overall project

Ice Breaking Activities

There are numerous activities or exercises which your facilitator can design into your session to help break the ice between the project partners. These might include everyone sharing their objectives for the partnering session, what they believe partnering might offer the project, or a game like "Howdy Partners" which is described below as a team-building activity. The objective is to get people comfortable with talking, listening, and interacting.

Ground rules for the session make it safe for participants to share openly and create an atmosphere which nurtures creativity

Making It Safe

Your facilitator will set ground rules for your workshop which will make it safe for participants to share openly. The ground rules also provide an atmosphere which nurtures creativity. Your facilitator will probably also give you a good overview of partnering so everyone in the group understands what they are charged with accomplishing during the workshop. An overview of partnering can be found in Part 2.

Getting to Know Each Other

Introductions
Getting to know the project members as professionals and as people is important. It is easier to get upset with a stranger, less so with someone you know and like. Introductions are often done in an interactive format, perhaps by interviewing one another, or breaking into small groups and discussing a table topic which is then shared with the entire partnering team. The introductions can help you gain knowledge about the roles and responsibilities of each person, as well as the background and experience each brings to the project.

Introductions help you understand the roles and responsibilities of the people on your partnering team — and lets you start knowing them as people

Getting Beyond Your Comfort Zone
It is important that you feel safe to openly share and create during the session, and that you get out of your comfort zone. You need to become open to seeing things in new ways, so that change is possible. Your facilitator may push to get you out of your comfort zone, often beginning with the introductions, by asking questions that let the group know you as a person, or by asking a provocative question. Whatever the technique, know that this discomfort is an important part of breaking down the barriers that bind us to the old ways of doing things and interacting in traditional roles.

Gaining Understanding

Understanding is Key to Creativity and Tolerance
Understanding leads to both creativity and tolerance. Cre-

Understanding leads to both creativity and tolerance

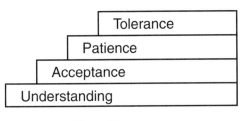

Figure 25

ativity is developed by seeking to truly understand what you and others need. With this understanding you can create options and solutions for fulfilling those needs. (There is more on this in Chapter 9.) Understanding is the first step in developing tolerance, so that differences don't routinely become conflicts or disputes, as the figure on the previous page shows. Understanding brings acceptance, and with acceptance there is patience, and this finally leads to tolerance. Developing understanding is important for your partnership.

Once you identify common interests, you can use them to develop momentum

Understanding Interests
Interests are those things which you need or want to happen as a result of this project or the partnering relationship. By sharing your organization's interests, all of the other participants will gain an understanding of your perspective, and they will be better able to help you obtain what you need during the project. This also will allow you to see where various team members have common interests and conflicting interests. The common interests are what you can use to push forward together and develop momentum. Conflicting interests are where problems are likely to arise. They are areas where you can creatively work to find solutions and options that address everyone's needs.

Sometimes your conflicts are polarities; polarities can not be solved in the normal sense of solving a problem, they must be managed

Sometimes our conflicting interests are polarities. Polarities are problems which are inherently connected to diametrically opposing issues. For example, a polarity exists between

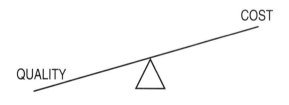

You have to manage cost and quality;
you can't have an unlimited amount of either.

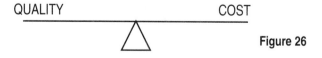

Figure 26

150

Polarity Chart

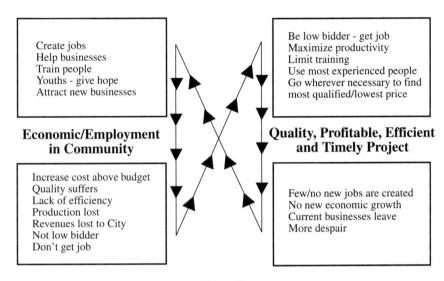

Figure 27

quality and cost. For the most part, everything that is done to build in quality adds to cost. So owners who want high quality and low-bid contractors who want low cost are dealing with a polarity. Polarities cannot be solved in the normal sense of solving a problem. Instead, they must first be identified, and then managed. To effectively manage a polarity there must be an understanding that both sides are right in their position and that there is no correct solution. In our example, managing the problem requires agreeing upon what constitutes an acceptable level of quality for an agreed-upon cost. Here are some examples.

The above polarity chart depicts a polarity encountered by city officials, members of the community, state officials, and the project team. The city wanted to receive economic benefits and employment for city residents from the project. The state wanted a quality, efficient, low cost, and timely project. Whatever was done to help one side achieve its objectives adversely affected the other side.

In order to create jobs and provide hope for the community, the city wanted the contractor to hire unskilled city residents

Each person walks into the partnering session with their own way of seeing the world, with their own set of paradigms

and train them. This would lead to higher costs and less efficiency for the selected contractor. Each contractor wanted to be the low bidder, maximize productivity, and make a profit by using the most experienced people he could find. This would lead to few, if any jobs being created, no economic growth, and more despair in the community. And around the loop we go again.

The more you act as a team, the more you become one

When you are dealing with a polarity you get stuck in an infinite loop — going around and around because of conflicting interests, never coming to a solution. The only way out of a polarity is to recognize it for what it is and begin to manage it by finding a way to optimally balance the two conflicting interests.

In the above case the group (city, state, and community) was successful in developing creative incentives to entice the contractors into meeting its needs.

Exploring Paradigms

Working closely with a group of strangers can be uncomfortable

Each person walks into the partnering session with his own way of seeing the world. We tend to see people as unique individuals until something occurs that makes us see them as a member of a group. Paradigms are the rules and regulations we carry with us about others. It is what we know to be true in general about a group: "Of course you are an exception, but in general this is how I see your type." By looking at the paradigms each of us has toward others, we can begin to see the biases affecting our view of our project teammates. This also serves as a warning that should things go sour, these biases probably will come pouring out onto the project like a tidal wave.

An example of a paradigm an owner might have toward contractors (not any individual contractor, but contractors in general, for this is where the true paradigm is found) is that contractors care only about profit. A contractor might have a paradigm about owners that they are all extremely bureaucratic. By understanding these paradigms you can work to choose new ones you want to use on this project, and you can work to discredit the reasons for the old paradigms.

Beginning to Act Like a Team

Team-building exercises bring the participants immediately into an activity in which they need to act as a team to be successful. I have seen an hour or two spent in team-building increase the level of trust and cooperation significantly. It stands to reason that the more you act like a team, the more you become one. Well-designed team-building activities can jump start your partnership. Far too often participants view team-building as "touchy-feely, waste of time" exercises, not understanding what is happening under the surface. Meeting a group of strangers and moving into activities in which you must work closely together can, at times, be uncomfortable; that is part of why it works. As I stated before, you must get out of your comfort zone in order to push beyond the status quo.

You must get out of your comfort zone in order to push beyond the status quo

Examples of Team-Building Activities

Here is a brief synopsis of four team-building activities with their objectives which have been used successfully with various groups. Facilitator's guides are available for all of these activities.

The Tower Project
This is a small group team-building activity in which the group seeks to build a tower using Tinkertoys®, meeting some specific performance requirements, and then examines how it performed as a team.

Howdy Partners
Based on the game of BINGO, Howdy Partners offers a lively way to get to know one another and reinforces partnering values throughout the workshop.

The Design/Build Game
The goal of this game is to understand the different perspectives of design and construction and how the two activities interface, along with learning to work together as a team toward a stated objective. Based on the Massachusetts

Institute of Technology's annual egg-drop event, the participants work with limited supplies to complete a successful mission...to save the egg. This is a great exercise for design/build projects.

Creativity in Construction

This exercise is designed to push the team into high gear for creative thinking. Teams over the past few years have literally created hundreds of ways to use a can of Coke®.

28

Learning Important Skills

The only way to discover the limtis of the possible is to go beyond them into the impossible.

Arthur C. Clarke

Understanding What Is Needed

From the pre-partnering process your facilitator understands the objectives you and your partnering team members have stated. Your facilitator also must understand the current issues and potential issues that stand in the way of the team meeting those objectives. With this understanding the facilitator can identify skills which will help the team members get from where they are now to where they want to be. Skills act like a bridge, allowing the partnering team members to work together toward accomplishing their objectives.

Identifying Skill Sets Needed

A skill set is an identifiable ability to do, perceive, or understand how to accomplish a specific task, such as negotiating, listening, benchmarking, or interacting. Skill sets might be developed to assure a common understanding, make up for a lack, or to push the team beyond its norms for excellence or creativity. Skills might be specific and designed to help in one particular area, such as effective recording/logging of project information. Or, they might be more general, designed to help in a broad range of areas and applications, such as effective leadership. No matter what your facilitator identifies as needed skills, they are to be de-

A skill set is an identifiable ability to do, perceive, or understand how to accomplish a specific task

veloped for the purpose of increasing the team's potential for success.

Designing the Training Required

Skills training usually takes place before the project team begins to discuss real project or relationship issues. There is a great deal of power in joint learning. In joint learning everyone learns the skills at the same time, and then practices the newly learned skills as they discuss project issues. This gives the team a common language and understanding for how to approach various issues.

There is a great deal of power in everyone learning the same skill at the same time, and then immediately using the skill to resolve project issues

Your facilitator is your guide in designing your training for skill-development. A skilled facilitator understands the elements of training design required to meet objectives and will create a module that enhances the partnering process and the team's effectiveness. A skilled facilitator can design your skill-building to fit the time allotted in the partnering session. This sometimes means your facilitator will incorporate your skills training into your team building exercises when time is limited.

Examples of Skills Training

The following are a few examples of what types of skills might be developed during your partnering workshop. These are but a few of the skills that your facilitator might select.

Negotiation skills can be of great assistance in dealing with conflict on the project

Negotiation
Effectively dealing with conflict on the project is important, and good negotiation skills can be of great assistance. Negotiation skills help you understand that people have both common and differing interests and needs, and that they can learn how to find common ground. Your team might learn how to negotiate everyday issues, or complex multi-party issues. Or, your team might learn the five different styles of negotiation, and when each is appropriate. Learning how to create options and solutions to problems is another skill of effective negotiation. Your facilitator has many areas from which to choose to meet your team's specific needs.

Communication

Communication is another multifaceted skill. In a communication skill-building module you might learn how to listen effectively, understand what your body language says about you and projects to others, how to speak so that you are understood, how to write effectively to communicate your message, or to understand how organizations communicate internally and externally. Communication is an excellent skill to work on as you discuss real project issues.

People/Motivation

Understanding what motivates you and others on your team, and what motivates people in general, is a valuable skill. Interpersonal skills, such as dealing with difficult people, various behavioral styles, differing leadership philosophies, and diversity might be selected to help your team become more effective.

Organizations

Each person who attends your workshop comes to it representing an organization or sub-organization. You may learn how to understand different organizational norms, styles, cultures, stages of growth, leadership styles, or values/reward systems. From understanding the similarities and differences, and the strengths and weaknesses, you can recognize and build on your strengths, utilize your differences for the project's benefit, and capitalize on your similarities for improved performance. Organizational understanding can go a long way toward assuring project success.

> *Communication is a multifaceted skill that includes listening, understanding body language, how to speak to be understood, and how to write effectively*

29

Solving Project Problems

The problems we face today cannot be solved at the same level of thinking we were at when we created them.

Albert Einstein

Solving problems together, in an atmosphere of creativity, openness, and trust does phenomenal things for your project. Every project has its challenges, as well as its opportunities. Far too often we spend our time and resources protecting our turf or position and end up exacerbating problems instead of solving them. During your partnering workshop you will have the opportunity to share with one another what you see as project issues and to work together toward their resolution.

Solving Problems Creatively

There are many problem-solving processes which your facilitator might select for you, but whichever is chosen should be built upon creativity, gaining understanding, and developing consensus. Creativity allows for the open flow of ideas and perspectives that might otherwise remain hidden. You cannot develop the best solutions until you have a real understanding of the problem and the needs of your partners.

Because you will spend a good portion of your time together working on solving project problems, this chapter will provide an example problem-solving process that you might use in your workshop.

Far too often we spend our time and resources protecting our position and placing blame rather than solving the problem

Identifying and Selecting Potential Problems

Expansion/Contraction or Convergence/Divergence Method

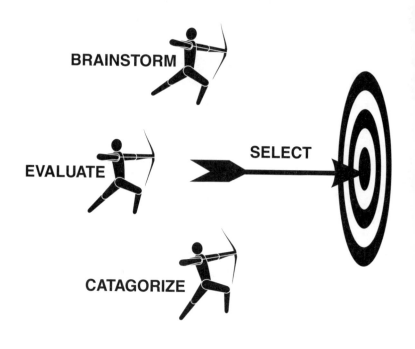

The expansion/ contraction model has two steps, first list all potential problems which come to mind by brainstorming, then evaluate and rank the list

Figure 28

The partnering team must first identify what are, or might become, project problems. Many of the team members may already have areas of concern. One method of problem-solving is the Expansion/Contraction Model. The team can utilize this model to help identify potential problems. The Expansion/Contraction Model has two steps and can be used on less complex problems, or when a quick decision is needed. The first step is to list all of the potential problems which come to your team's mind, without judgment, a free-flowing brainstorming of ideas. This is the expansion portion of the model. Here the right side of the brain is called upon to come up with ideas, subjectively. After the group has exhausted its list of ideas and has recorded the ideas on a flip chart, step two begins. In step two the group evokes the left, analytical brain to evaluate and rank the list. Some of the items may fit together and develop into a category. Not all items on the list are of equal importance, so the group now must select which items are most important, and rank them. The group is asked which potential problem is most important to the project's success, which is the second most important, and so on. Now the team has an agreed-upon list of project problems, in rank order, which can now begin to be resolved.

The four step problem-solving model was developed from a combination of decision-making and creative-thinking models

Solutions can be found using a similar method. Ideas for solving any given problem are identified, without judgment (brainstorming), and then the group selects the best solutions from those offered, ranking them, and finally, agreeing upon implementation.

Four Steps to Creative Problem Solving

This four-step model was developed from a combination of decision-making and creative-thinking models, and compressed into four steps. Your team will have developed its list of the most important problems, each of which will be taken through the four-step creative problem-solving process.

Step One: State the Problem

We begin seeking solutions without fully understanding the problem, and frequently different members of your group will have different understandings of what the problem is. So the first step is to agree upon what the problem is by stating it clearly and unequivocally. The more specific you are, the better chance you will have for really creating a solution.

The first step is to state the problem — everyone must agree what the problem really is

Step Two: List All the Facts

By listing all of the facts you know about the problem, you can explore its many facets. You may find that there are two or three main areas where the problem occurs. Or you may find that the problem lies only with one organization. Whatever you discover, you will be more enlightened about the nature of the problem, its cause, and its potential solution.

Step Three: Create Solutions and Options

Now you are ready to seek solutions that will specifically solve the problem you stated, and now better understand. Your team will create as many solutions as it can, and then select the one, two, or three that will best solve the problem. Allow yourselves to be creative; breakthroughs don't happen from staying safe, they come from the fringes.

By listing all the facts you know about the problem you will better understand the nature of the problem, its cause(s), and its potential solution

An example of such thinking occurred during a session where the team was seeking to find a way to remove ice from power lines to keep power from being interrupted. For years the linemen had to drive their trucks into desolate areas, often at night, climb the power poles and shake the ice off the lines. This was not only dangerous but also took a long time.

The team had become frustrated, and toward the end of the second day had come back to the conclusion that climbing the poles and shaking them, as they always had done, was still the best solution. Frustrated, one team member said, "Why don't we get some of those bears out there to climb up the pole and shake off the ice?" Another person said, "Yeah, their climbing would do it, but how do you get them there when you need them?" Still another person said, "Well, we could hang a honey pot at the top of the pole and that would attract the bears up the pole." But another objected that there were other critters who would eat the honey before the bears got to it.

Create as many solutions as you can, without judging them — be as outrageous as you can

One of the participants had been a helicopter pilot in Vietnam, and she said that they used to be able to fly over small areas and drop off items. Maybe they could fly over the poles and place the honey pots at the tops, just when they were needed. All of a sudden there was a flash of insight. The downward thrust of the helicopter was strong enough to remove the ice from the lines. And so a breakthrough was found - not from a clear analytical process, but from frustration and giddiness.

Step Four: Select the Best

The final step is to select the best solution(s). After you and the team have explored those solutions that you feel might work, you can choose the one(s) that the you feel will have the best chance of resolving the problem. Many times your problem has several facets, so your solution(s) will as well. For example, a problem in timeliness which might include response time, submission time, inspection, supplies, and so on. Your solution(s), too, must address each facet of the problem identified by the team.

The final step is to select the best solution

For an exploration of several case studies of partnered projects I highly recommend The Associated General Contractors of America's book *Partnering, Changing Attitudes in Construction*. It is filled with interesting cases that will provide ideas and insights for you partnerings.

30

Creating a Mission and Collective Goals

There is no such thing as a self-made man. You reach your goals only with the help of others.

George Shinn

Creating a Project Vision

Taking a look at your project from the viewpoint of what would make it an ideal project is where we begin in creating a project vision. You may already know what your concerns are and have a general idea of what you would like from this project, but now is the time to look at what is possible on this project.

Your collective vision for the project paints a picture of what you all want "ideally" to have happen during, or as a result of, working together on this project. Your vision will include areas of agreement and areas of difference. For example contractors might say they wish to make a profit, and public agency representatives might say they wish to come in under budget. This would normally be considered an area of conflict. But, if both of these ideals are included in your vision, you will then explore what each really means as you create your mission, goals and actions, and come to agreement on how to achieve both.

A vision can be a statement, a list of words and phrases, or one or more paragraphs which describe your ideal project

A vision can be a statement, a list of words and phrases, or one or more paragraphs which describe your ideal project. It matters only that what you create truly depicts what would be your ideal. I have noticed that people who have attended several partnering sessions, and have developed visions and missions for other projects, bring with them a limited vision for what is possible. They already have the words they always use. This truly limits creativity and sticks the group into an old vision. Each project should be looked at separately, freshly, and creatively. The same old words become lackluster and meaningless over time. There is no growth, stagnation begins to set in, and partnering begins to seem boring.

Using the same words you've used on other projects limits your vision, making it lackluster and meaningless

Another caveat is that you must create a vision that is physically, politically and financially possible. If you are starting a project in the dead of winter, and wish for no bad weather, then your vision will not be seen as credible, and perhaps even as a joke. Your vision should incorporate what you truly want to have happen on your project, pushing toward what's possible, or even improbable, but not impossible. Striving for the impossible will only diffuse the team's energy. You may have to spend some time discussing what is possible, what is improbable, and what is impossible to come to a common understanding and agreement.

Your Team's Mission

Your mission statement is developed from your vision. Your mission statement is what your team is committing itself to accomplishing. The partnering team works collectively to incorporate into their mission statement those aspects of their vision they feel are the most important. The mission statement's development and acceptance must be consensual. Everyone must agree that if the team were to read the mission statement at the end of the project, and could honestly say "Yes, we accomplished this," then this will have been a great project for everyone. When the team can agree, then you have a good mission statement.

The mission is the partnering team's target, what the team is always heading toward

The mission is the partnering team's target. From the moment the members agree that this is their mission, the team is always heading toward accomplishing it. The mission can also act as a touchstone for making the myriad of decisions that must be made during the project. You can weigh possible decisions against your mission and see which one moves you closer toward achieving it. If everyone on the project knows, understands and buys-in to your mission, you have a powerful management tool for keeping your project on track. Here are a couple of examples of mission statements:

From an air quality retrofit project:
The Project Partnering Team is committed to developing a model project that sets the standard for future work. We will accomplish this through cooperation, communication, teamwork and by developing common goals for the installation of emissions retrofits on units K-11 and K-12 at the Hinkley Compressor Station. We will do this at the lowest life-cycle cost, ahead of schedule, under budget, safely, and with a minimum of disruptions to operations. We will meet the requirements of reliability, operability and satisfy the regulatory agencies. We will achieve this with no unresolved disputes, in a flexible, responsive, professional manner, leading to an enjoyable, lasting partnership.

The mission statement can act as a touchstone for the myriad of decisions that must be made during the project

From a building project
The City has undertaken a process to improve the public workspace, to enhance the image of the city, and create a new public sense of pride in the downtown.

Our mission is to provide the design and construction of such facilities consistent with the city's mission, program documents, and design/build competition. Working together as a team, we will provide these services in an enjoyable, timely, educational, profitable, and spectacular manner for all stakeholders.

Project Objectives
    Complete the project within budget
    Create a legacy of fair dealings (no litigation)
    To complete the project on time
    To provide high quality
    To be profitable for all
    To create "raving fans" who love the project
        User friendly
        Public satisfaction
        That there is genuine achievement for the community in employment
        and contracting
    For the project to be enjoyable (a smooth process)
    To be award-winning
    To become a model design/build project (set standards for future projects)

Goals are aimed at accomplishing your mission

Setting Goals

Your goals are aimed at accomplishing your mission. Chapter 29 was about the project's problems and potential problems, those things that might be in the way of the team accomplishing its mission. Once identified and prioritized, and the top few selected as being most critical to the success of the project, the team moves through the creative problem solving process, which results in selection of the best solutions for each problem. Now it is time to take those solutions and turn them into goals for the project. This process builds in direction and commitment.

Take the solutions to your problems and turn them into goals

Figure 29

Through this strategic process the team develops congruence of purpose. In this way each agreed-upon action that is taken leads toward the accomplishment of a goal, a goal that was a result of a problem, one seen as being central, one that impaired the team's ability to accomplish its mission and ultimately achieve its vision of an ideal project.

Goals need to be as specific as possible — who will do what and by when.

Goals need to be specific, so that you and your team members will know if and when they are accomplished. Broad, general goals, such as "have open communication" are so vague that no one will be able to know if they were accomplished. A goal of "weekly meetings are to be held on Tuesdays with a preset agenda" is specific enough that everyone will know whether it is happening or not.

Goals offer the team an opportunity to develop a good deal of trust. If you agree to a certain goal, and you go out and do what you said you would, then the team's level of trust is greatly increased. On the other hand, if you set a goal and say you will do something, and you fail to do so, then the team's level of trust can be greatly hurt.

To help assure that your goals are specific enough, you can develop an action plan for each.

Developing Action Plans

Key Issue #1: Compliance at the lowest lifecycle cost - competitiveness of plant

Sub-Issue #1A: Develop stategy and identify issues

Action Plan #1A1: Assemble data

	WHAT	WHO	WHEN
1	Existing studies	JMR	Now
2	Economic factor	CJW	11/1/94
3	S-Burner results	JMR/DPT	12/1/94
4	Drawings	CRH	11/1/94
5	Permit requirements and codes	MEW	11/1/94
6	Test data (previous)	JMR	11/1/94

Action Plan #1A2: Constraints and performance requirements

	WHAT	WHO	WHEN
1	Site walkdowns	BDW	1/15/95
2	Identify constraints with plant	All with BDW	1/15/95
3	Identify additional test requirements	B&W	1/20/95
4	Identify performance requirements	BDW (all)	1/25/95

Action Plan #1A3: Decision model

	WHAT	WHO	WHEN
1	Develop a decision tree	BDW	2/1/95

Figure 30

An action plan lists the steps you will take to achieve your goals

An action plan describes the steps or tasks required to accomplish an agreed-upon goal. It then identifies the person responsible for accomplishing each step/task, and a date by which it is to be completed. In essence, this process breaks down each goal into the specific action steps required to be taken. It assures that there is no obscure goal that no one knows how to accomplish. These actions are agreed upon by the partnering team, just as the goals were. New actions may be needed as the project progresses. Measurement of your success in achieving your goals, and identifying new problems as they arise also is required. This is why evaluating your progress is so important, and will be discussed in Step 5.

An action plan will ensure that there is no obscure goal that no one knows how to accomplish

31

Developing a Dispute Resolution Process

> *When we chose to live by the spirit rather than the letter of the law —*
> *offering our hand and word as our bond — we distinguish ourselves. When*
> *we don't, we give up treasured values and mirror the dark, litigious side of*
> *construction.*
>
> Charles E. Cowan
> *Partnering, a Strategy for Excellence*

Learning how to resolve disputes between the team members during the project is an important component of the partnering process. In this chapter I describe what you might experience at your session.

Elevation of an Issue

Over the past several years one dispute-resolution process has become classic in partnering — Elevation of an Issue. Some may refer to it as Escalation of an Issue. I find that an unfortunate term as our goal is not to escalate an issue, but to resolve it. There are many other forms of dispute-resolution processes which your partnering team can use on your project, but Elevation of an Issue has become well-known and accepted. In Chapter 41 you will find more information about the trends in Alternative Dispute Resolution for construction.

Elevation of an Issue has become the classic dispute resolution

Goes with the Flow

What makes Elevation of an Issue so popular is that it mirrors the flow of the hierarchical/bureaucratic organization , which usually is the organizational style of one or more of the project partners. Bureaucratic organizations are hierarchical by design. That means that power and authority rise within the organization, as does the ability to make decisions. Elevation of an Issue works within this style, moving up the organization's levels until an issue is resolved. In this way disputes are resolved by working within the existing parameters of the organization's structure. A dispute resolution process which works counter to the existing culture is difficult to implement, and, therefore, less effective. This is not to say that bureaucratic organizations can't work to improve their empowerment of people at lower levels; they can and should, but many times public organizations are prohibited by law or statute from doing so. And change of this sort comes slowly, so it is better for your project to push for improvement and go with the flow.

Elevation of an Issue works well since most organizations are hierarchical by design

Others are Championed Through

With Elevation of an Issue the two (or three) main players are at the top of the chart. All other project participants line up behind these main players. For example, behind the owner might be the architect, engineer(s), construction manager, or funding agency. Behind the contractor might be the subcontractors and suppliers. It is the role of the contractor or owner to champion each of their team's disputes through the process. This is a commitment that is made by all par-

The process starts within each organization at the closest level possible to the problem

	Architect/Engineer	Suppliers/Subs	
	Owner	**Contractor**	**Time to Elevate**
Level I	Assistant Supervisor or Engineer	Foreman	Field: by end of shift Contract: up to 1 week
Level II	Project Superintendent or Project Engineer	Superintendent General Foreman Project Manager	Field: up to 8 hours Contract: up to 1 week
Level III	Construction Manager	Project Manager Area Manager	Field: up to 2 days Contract: up to 1 week
Level IV	Project Director or Program Manager	Area Manager Owner	Field: up to 3 days Contract: up to 2 weeks
Level V	Director Facilities Dept or Manager, Capital Programs	Owner	Field: up to 3 days Contract: up to 2 weeks
Level VI	Board of Supervisors	Owner	Select next form of ADR

Figure 31

ticipants. So, from the example Elevation of an Issue table, a subcontractor who has a dispute with the owner would go to the contractor's foreman to begin the resolution process, and progress through the people named at each level until the dispute is resolved.

How It Works

The process starts at the lowest level possible for each organization. This is usually at the source, the field level. For our example this is the assistant supervisor for field issues or the engineer for administrative issues on the owner's side, and the foreman on the contractor's side. Remember, the issue might be between the A/E and a subcontractor. In such an instance the A/E, subcontractor, along with the assistant supervisor and engineer meet to try and resolve the dispute. If they fail to resolve the issue, it moves up each organization's chain-of-command.

It is acceptable for the people at one level to immediately decide that the issue needs to be elevated to the next level

An issue is allowed to stay at each level for an agreed-upon amount of time before it is elevated to the next level. In our example, it is to be elevated by the end of the shift if it is a field problem, and by the end of one week for contract issues. The nature of the dispute may be such that the people at Level I agree within seconds that they cannot resolve it. It this case it is automatically and immediately bumped up to the next level.

Many times information is being gathered about a dispute. When this occurs the information should be flowing up and down both organizations simultaneously, so that direction and authority may come down from the higher levels to Level I, where the dispute can be resolved. Both sides do not have to agree that the issue needs to be elevated. One side can determine that it is at an impasse and can move the dispute up to the next level. In our example it would move to Level II and stay for the agreed-upon time, then move to Level III, and so on, if still unresolved. It is important that information continue to flow up and down both organizations, so that when the issue reaches the third, fourth and fifth levels they are fully versed in the problems.

As you move up the organization, you remove some of the emotional attachment to the problem — allowing for a solution

This process allows issues to be resolved quickly, moving them along so they don't fester, and helps prevent people from digging their heels in to support their position. As you move up in the organizations you usually also move away from the day-to-day management of the project, to others who are less emotionally involved and theoretically more objective.

One way to undermine the dispute process is for people to go around the person they are supposed to work with because they don't like them

You can see from Level VI that if the issue is not resolved within the time frame allotted, another form of alternative dispute resolution will be selected (or a previously selected ADR process will take place). Chapter 41 outlines some of the ADR choices available for your use.

One way to undermine your dispute process is for people to go around those they don't like or disagree with. For example, suppose the contractor's foreman talks with the owner's assistant supervisor, doesn't like what he says, and then goes directly to the project director, skipping the project superintendent and the construction manager because he likes the project director, and the project director solves the problem. Your process will be destroyed quickly. What the project director should do is ask the foreman "What did the construction manager say?" When the director hears that the foreman never talked with the construction manager, nor does the CM know anything about the issue since the project superintendent was never contacted, the director sends the dispute back to the assistant supervisor to be elevated to Level II. He does not solve it without going through the proper levels. However, the project director may explicitly give the people at Level I or II the authority to solve it.

A dispute is a disagreement between two or more people — it's that simple

Identifying a Dispute

Many times the dispute process fail because no one uses it. When I ask why, it becomes clear that no one really understood what a dispute was. *A dispute is a disagreement between two or more people*. It's that simple. A dispute that goes on for some period of time with no movement toward resolution is an impasse. At impasse people are usually entrenched in their positions and want to WIN, or at least prove that they are right and you are wrong. So your dispute process is what keeps you from impasse, solving disagreements before they escalate (that is why you should elevate an issue, not escalate it). Any of the parties involved in an issue can tell the other parties they feel the issue is a disagreement and move it into the dispute process. Let the process work for you. It will preserve relationships and resolve disputes in timely fashion.

Another problem occurs when issues are not elevated because to do so makes people at the lower levels feel as if they failed, or because they really want to maintain control at their level. I have seen disputes stay at Level I for four to five months. War was the result — no cooperation, no communication, loss of production, not to mention lots of stress. It is the responsibility of upper management to make sure it is safe for lower-level people to elevate issues. It is the responsibility of lower-level people to honestly work to solve issues at their level before they elevate them.

It is the responsibility of upper management to make sure it is safe for lower level people to elevate an issue

It takes a little time to learn to clearly recognize a dispute, but when you do, you will have a tool that will go a long way toward insuring your project's success.

For Dispute Resolution - Not Problem Solving

Remember, this process is not for normal communications; it is not a process for problem-solving; it is for resolving disagreements.

32

Signing the Partnering Agreement

The antidote to self-interest is to commit and to find cause. To commit to something outside of ourselves. To be part of creating something we care about so we can endure the sacrifice, risk, and adventure that commitment entails. This is the deeper meaning of service.

Peter Block
Stewardship

Well, you've done it. You've come together, gotten to know each other, concentrated on your project, and envisioned a great future together. Now it's time to sign your partnering agreement.

Your Personal Commitment

At the end of your partnering session you will perform the final ritual of partnering, signing your partnering agreement (or charter). Some groups have purchased special pens for each member to use in signing the partnering agreement or have celebrated with a toast of sparkling apple cider to acknowledge the beginning of a new relationship. This ceremony celebrates all that you have done together during the session and confirms your personal commitment to work toward accomplishing what you have created together. This includes your:

■ Vision/Mission
■ Goals/Actions
■ Dispute Resolution Process
■ Evaluation Process

Your commitment includes embracing the partnering values, working to continue developing as a team, and to practicing the partnering skills you have learned.

At the end of your partnering session you will perform the final ritual of partnering, signing your partnering agreement

Partnering is not an event — it is a mind-set. You cannot just attend your partnering workshop and expect everything miraculously to be better. It takes continuous effort. But now you know what you need to do, together, to make your project the best it can be.

When you and your fellow project team members sign your partnering agreement you are committing your personal efforts to making the partnership work and grow over the duration of the project.

Your partnering agreement is a personal agreement, not a legal document

Not a Legal Document

Your partnering agreement is a personal commitment, not a legal document. Thousands of building and construction projects have been partnered, and to my knowledge, no partnering agreement has ever become a legal problem. This includes hundreds or even thousands of private and public organizations which have had their legal counsel review partnering and its subsequent agreements. If your legal staff has questions, have them talk to other organizations' legal staff, or, as an alternative, have them review some of the American Bar Association's Construction Section's many articles about partnering and its positive impact on the industry.

Sample Partnering Agreement

Good Government County and abc General Contractor
Housing Replacement Project
Partnering Session
June 16-17, 1996

abc
General Contractor

MISSION

The Good Government County Housing Replacement Project Partnering Team is committed to creating a safe, secure, humane housing environment for kids and staff, on time and within budget by:

- A cooperative team effort
- Trusting one another
- Open and timely communication
- Safe working conditions
- Team ownership and resolution of problems
- Quality, mutual profit, and pride in work

KEY ISSUES and GOALS

Key Issue #1   **Participation of general contractor and subs in design problem resolution**

Goals
- 1.1   Pre-construction and pre-component meetings shall be held and everyone shall be prepared.
- 1.2   Modify RFI form with point person of issuance CM
- 1.3   All submittals shall be processed in a timely manner

Key Issue #2   **Subcontractor coordination**

Sub Issue 2A   Leadership by General Contractor
Goals
- 2A.1   Develop clear statement of responsibilities and consensus by team
- 2A.2   Clear and timely communication
- 2A.3   Set tone of project (cooperation)
- 2A.4   Execute and facilitate problem solving

Sub Issue 2B   Submittals
Goals
- 2B.1   The general will identify submittals required
- 2B.2   Tie into schedule and prioritize
- 2B.3   General to review prior to submission
- 2B.4   Sub to assemble package per contract requirements
- 2B.5   Submit accurate coordination drawings

Figure 32

STEP FIVE

FOLLOW THROUGH WITH YOUR COMMITMENTS

33

Executing and Communicating Your Commitments

There can be no friendship without confidence, and no confidence without integrity.

Samuel Johnson

Fulfilling your commitments to each other and to your project will provide not only the benefits associated with the commitments, but will continue to build the trust formed in the partnering session. This trust-building provides the foundation to set and achieve even more ambitious goals. During your partnering workshop you have co-created your mission, goals, and action plans. Now it is time to execute your plan.

Building On Trust - the Cost/Trust Relationship

The foundation on which your cooperative relationship is based is trust. Working to continue building trust can have a dramatically positive impact on your project. Intuitively, it seems that building trust between project partners makes sense for the project. The Construction Industry Institute (CII) has found empirical evidence that there is a definite Cost/Trust relationship. The more trust you develop, the less the cost; the less trust you have, the higher the cost. The cost/trust curve on the next page shows how this might work on your job.

The foundation on which your cooperative relationship is built is trust

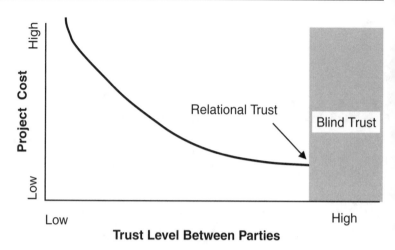

Source: CII Special Report 24-1, "The Cost/Trust Relationship," November 1994

Figure 33

Trust will be a result of following through with the commitments you make at the partnering workshop

Trust will be a result of your following-through with the commitments you made during your partnering workshop, and communicating this follow-through back to your partners. Personal integrity will go a long way toward helping to build a spirit of trust between the project partners. You must also recognize the follow-through of your partners.

Identifying and Overcoming Potential Barriers

What potential barriers might you encounter within you own organization?

As you begin to think about putting your partnership into action, what potential barriers might you encounter within your own organization? Is your organization's culture such that trust and cooperation are a part of your everyday work life? Does information flow freely and swiftly and are decisions made at the field level? If not, what can you do to bridge the gap?

EXERCISE:

Use the following space to think through potential barriers to the success of your partnership and the partnering values. What are methods for overcoming each?

Potential Barriers To Partnering   Ideas/Methods For Overcoming

1 _____   _____

_____   _____

_____   _____

2 _____   _____

_____   _____

_____   _____

3 _____   _____

_____   _____

_____   _____

4 _____   _____

_____   _____

_____   _____

Upwards of ninety percent of the people on your project will not have attended the partnering workshop — each needs to be made to feel like a partner on the project

Getting Buy-in and Communicating Your Commitments

Upwards to ninety percent of the people who will work on your project will not have attended the partnering workshop. They will not know what has happened at the session, or what has been agreed to. Yet, they will play a major role in executing the commitments. Each person working on your project needs to feel like they are a partner and an important part of fulfilling the commitments you have developed. As with leadership, partnering is best done by example. When project personnel who did not participate in the partnering session notice from the behavior of the workshop participants that this project is not "business-as-usual"

Those who do attend the partnering workshop are responsible for bringing the others on-board

they will likely get caught up in the esprit de corps and join in.

Given the above, then, those who attend the partnering workshop are responsible for bringing the others within their organization and sphere of influence on-board as partners. If you are the general contractor, your sphere of influence includes not only your crew members, but your subcontractors and suppliers. If you are the owner, architect or engineer, your sphere of influence includes your personnel along with your sub-consultants.

Those who attend the partnering workshop are responsible for bringing others on-board

Far too often the commitments made during the partnering session do not get communicated to the field crews, sub-consultants, suppliers, or subcontractors. The partners are rolling along feeling that the project is off to a good start, but the field staff, subs and sub-consultants who did not attend the partnering session start off just as always. Often resentment grows when the partners begin to interfere in what the field personnel, subcontractors and sub-consultants feel is "their" job.

The best time to bring the crews and others on-board is at the beginning. I have written a small booklet titled *Howdy Partners* which is designed specifically to explain to those people who will work on your project, but did not attend the partnering workshop, that they are working on a "partnered" project and that they are an important part of the partnering team. After all, they will be charged with actually building the project. It takes them through an overview of what partnering is. There is a place on the back cover of the booklet for a laminated card with the project's mission statement and goals.

The best time to bring others on-board is at the beginning

You might choose to hold an internal meeting to discuss what occurred at the partnering workshop, explain how the mission and goals will be implemented, and get input. On one job the owner created a short video tape which explained their vision of the completed project, described the partnering spirit and explained the project team's mission and goals. Every person who came to the site to work watched that video. The same thing could be done with an

EXERCISE:

How will you gain buy-in, and communicate your commitments?

1 _____

_____

_____

2 _____

_____

_____

3 _____

_____

_____

You must get everyone to buy into the commitments you have made

audio tape. Posting your partnering agreement in your project meeting room helps to remind the team of their commitments.

The point is, you must get everyone to buy into the commitments you have made, and to understand that they are an integral part of fulfilling the project mission. The sooner everyone understands this the better. Not doing this effectively can cause an early breakdown in your partnering effort.

Posting your partnering agreement in your project meeting room helps to remind the team of their commitments

Developing a Plan for Executing Your Partnering Agreement

You have worked to overcome internal barriers to partnering, and devised ways to communicate and gain buy-in to the partnering mission and goals, both of which are a part of developing your plan for implementing your partnering agreement. Last, you need to decide who will do what. What are the roles and responsibilities for each of the people in your organization or sub-organization in fulfilling the partnering agreement? Each person should clearly understand what his role is and responsibilities are so he can go forward and fulfill his duties.

Uncertainty about who is responsible, at what level of authority certain decisions may be made, what is really meant by a particular goal, and who to talk to in other organizations all cause confusion and diffuse the partnering effort.

Your plan for implementing your partnering agreement should include:

- Identify barriers to partnering, and how will we overcome each.
- Communicate our commitments and gain buy-in from all those in our sphere of influence.
- Identify who is responsible for what, and what are the specific roles and responsibilities for each person.

34

Evaluating Progress and Measuring Success

Partnership acknowledges that we are capable of defining for ourselves the rules and yardsticks by which we live and work.

Peter Block
Stewardship

This chapter covers developing a process for evaluating and measuring your progress in meeting your goals and mission, and maintaining the partnering spirit.

What Gets Measured Gets Done

You have come together and worked hard during your partnering workshop to diagnose and prescribe solutions to the problems, and potential problems, that you will face on your project. You have developed action plans for their implementation. It is equally important that you develop a process for measuring and evaluating your progress.

Caution! Lack of attention to measuring and evaluating progress is a threat to meeting your partnering goals and to the success of your project. Most teams do a poor job at measuring and evaluating how they are doing. Over time, commitments erode, and the team members don't remember what they were working to accomplish. Things change, too, and the issues which appeared to be the critical path to success are now different. For all of these reasons it is important to keep your partnership alive and well by periodically examining how you are doing.

Most teams do a poor job at measuring and evaluating how they are doing

If you don't identify and evaluate performance measurements for each partnering goal, it will be very difficult to proactively identify the need for mid-project corrections. By asking your team members (and other project members) their opinion you are reminding them that partnering is important and worth their attention.

What to Measure

Measuring how well you are doing toward accomplishing your mission is a good place to begin your evaluation effort

The Mission

Your mission statement is the target for which you are aiming. Your mission statement is the touchstone for success. Everyone agreed at the partnering workshop that if you accomplished your mission, the project would be a success. Measuring how you are doing toward its accomplishment is a good place to begin your evaluation effort.

The Goals/Actions

You will have developed goals and an action plan to accomplish each goal that the team agreed was critical to accomplishing the mission. Measuring your progress in accomplishing each goal and assuring that the actions are taking place is the next step.

The Partnering Spirit/Effort

Partnering is more than a mission and goals. It is a spirit of trust and cooperation, so that communication flows freely and people share their ideas and problems openly. Measuring how the team is "growing" the partnering spirit, and the amount of effort being made to assure success, are vital measuring points.

How the team is growing the partnering spirit is a vital measurement point

New issues

New issues are bound to come up as the project moves along. Issues that are challenges to accomplishing the mission, a goal, or an action will need to be addressed right away. Issues that are challenges to the partnering spirit or effort also will surface, and need to be dealt with.

Successes

It is equally important to measure and acknowledge what is going well. Don't build your partnership only on what is going wrong and the new challenges the team is facing; build on your successes. Partnering really works when the team focuses on the positive; what's going right, what problems have been solved, where are we ahead of schedule, etc. Those who are demonstrating cooperation and achieving effective results should be acknowledged and rewarded by the team.

How Often Will You Measure?

It is important to decide how often you will check in with each other and take an objective view of the project, the partnership and your issues. Far too often partnering teams do not evaluate often enough to be able to make required adjustments before damage occurs. Decide how often you will measure your progress by looking at what it will take to keep your commitments and level of trust growing.

Far too often partnering teams do not evaluate often enough to make required adjustments

Many groups choose to check in once or twice a month, in a more informal fashion. Other groups select a milestone at which they will sit down and evaluate their progress. Some others decide they will review how they are doing quarterly. The rule of thumb is that evaluation needs to happen often enough so that adjustments can be made to minimize or avoid impacts to project goals.

How Will You Measure?

As stated before, there are informal and more formal ways to measure your partnering progress. Below are some of the more common ways partnering teams measure. No matter which method the partnering team decides to use, specific objectives for measurement need to be developed.

There are both formal and informal ways to measure progress

Agenda Item
Most projects hold weekly meetings. Many partnering teams place partnering on the agenda. This might be each week or once a month. Either way, the project team is reviewing how well it is accomplishing its partnering objectives on a regular basis. Since not all of the partners attend every weekly meeting, often a specific meeting is selected each month to discuss the partnership. All the partners commit to attending this meeting.

Monthly/Bimonthly Partnering Meeting

Many partnering teams prefer a separate meeting specifically held to discuss the partnership. This meeting is usually attended by all the partners, but occasionally there is a meeting limited to upper management. At either type of meeting there is discussion and evaluation of the mission, goals/actions, brainstorming of solutions to new issues, and recognition of successes. It is important that the team focuses on partnering and team process issues at these meetings, and not fall into the common trap of turning the meetings into problem-solving sessions for the latest technical issue(s) on the project. There is also often a social flavor to this meeting, as it is often held over lunch or dinner.

Written Survey

Some teams feel that they want to have a quantifiable measure of their progress. They choose to send out a survey, collect and tally the results, and use this information to measure progress. There are pros and cons to this approach. Pros are that it is anonymous; people can speak their minds on the survey and no one will know who it came from. Some partners feel this gives them a much better feel for what is really going on. The cons are that few of the surveys sent out are ever returned, leaving the team wondering what is going on (and potentially indicating a lack of commitment). A sample survey is recreated at the end of this chapter that, for the example project, indicates areas needing attention.

Monthly Social Event

A brown-bag lunch, a barbecue, or basketball game also can serve as a means for measuring progress and building the team effort. Many teams get together and discuss the partnership at a shared social event. This has proven to be an effective and beneficial way to evaluate progress. Most often the partnering organizations alternate responsibility for setting up the monthly event.

Who Will Measure Progress?

Someone must take the responsibility for measuring progress. There are two schools of thought on who is best-suited for this. One school believes that the owner's and

> *Many partnering teams prefer a separate meeting expressly for the purpose of discussing the partnership*

> *Someone must take the responsibility for measuring progress*

architect's project manager and the contractor's superintendent are best-suited to know what goes on day-to-day and can best monitor progress. Another school believes that someone possibly more objective should measure progress, someone not involved in the day-to-day operations of the job. I have seen it work both ways. Measurement could be done by someone appointed to the task who then communicates the results at the appointed meeting. The fact that someone does the measuring is more important than who does it. It takes commitment. There is more about this in Chapter 35.

What Will You Do with the Information Gathered?

Far too often information is gathered in the form of surveys, interviews, discussions, or brainstorming sessions and then nothing is done to disseminate the information or to use it to make the adjustments required to become successful.

Deciding exactly what you will do with the information gathered from your evaluation process is critical to keeping the partnership alive and well. This can be decided easily at your partnering workshop, or at the first evaluation meeting.

Making sure the partnership grows and flourishes is far too important to leave to chance. That is why the next chapter describes selecting partnering champions.

The information you gather through surveys, interviews, discussions, or brainstorming is wasted unless you do something with it

Example Evaluation Form

Name/Title: _Contractor and Owner_   Date: _____

Project: _XYZ Phase 2_

Please evaluate inter-organizational performance during the past month.

1) Key Issue #1 Safety

Poor   Excellent
1   2   3   ④   5   6

Comments:
On-going improvement needed

2) Key Issue #2a Cooperation; Respect; Trust

Poor   Excellent
1   2   ③   4   5   6

Comments:
Job delays causing stain on everyone - improvement needed.

3) Key Issue #2b Pro-Active Problem Solving

Poor   Excellent
1   ②   3   4   5   6

Comments:
Contractor feels owner isn't pro-active; owner feels contractor isn't (contractor gave good reasons for their concerns)

4) Key Issue #3 Dispute Resolution

Poor   Excellent
1   2   ③   4   5   6

Comments:
Contractor sees the right-of-way delay as being unresolved. Owner feels contractor hasn't followed up on submitted potential claims.

5) Key Issue #4 Design Support

Poor   Excellent
1   2   ③   4   5   6

Comments:
Design support is lacking on existing roadway plans. Not fast enough on bridge stuff either.

6) Key Issue #5 How We Deal With 3rd Parties

Poor   Excellent
1   2   3   ④   5   6

Comments:
OK, especially considering all the problems caused by third parties.

Figure 34

35

Selecting Partnering Champions

People who say it cannot be done should not interrupt those who are doing it.

Jack Canfield and Mark Victor Hansen
Chicken Soup for the Soul

A Partnering Champion

A partnering champion is someone who watches over the partnership. They are charged with doing all they can to make sure the partnership is successful. They are asked to take an objective view from time-to-time to make sure things are on track. They are in charge of the care and feeding of the partnership and are empowered to do what it takes to make it work.

Selecting Your Partnering Champions

The American Heritage Dictionary defines a champion as "one who defends a cause." When selecting your partnering champions it is important to remember this definition and select those people from each organization who most believe in partnering. It can be devastating to select someone who knows little about partnering and is convinced that it won't work.

> *A champion is "one who defends a cause"*

One person should be selected for each of the main project organizations, the owner/construction manager, architect or engineer and the general contractor. The best champions are those who volunteer, but appointed champions can also be good if the team is confident of the champion's commitment to partnering. The partnering champion is most effective when he/she has effective people skills and a positive attitude.

Your partnering champion(s) may or may not be the same individual(s) performing your partnering progress evaluation.

Ways to Champion Your Partnering

Select a time/day to step back and see
Select a time each day or one day each week during which you will step back for an objective view of the project and the partnership. The idea is to make checking in a habit; you are regularly taking a litmus test for how things are going.

Keep a log of things going well
Keeping a log of what is going right and who is contributing to the project's success allows you to praise the people doing things well. If you reward them, with your kind word, a T-shirt, coffee mug, etc., they are much more likely to repeat the good behavior. Your log also serves to remind you, and everyone else, when things get challenging, that not everything is going wrong.

Keep a list of things to improve
Watching out for potential problems with relationships, tracking project issues that aren't being solved, and listing potential challenges, go a long way toward proactively making corrections before they become problems. Many times someone knows something is going to happen, but they are so caught up in the day-to-day activities of building the job that they don't do anything to stop it. The partnering champion can intervene and stop problems before they happen — especially relationship problems.

Read the mission statement every day
Your mission statement is what you are aiming to accomplish. By reading it each day, you can make sure you are watching out for things that might block its accomplishment. Having it in front of you and all your team members is an effective way to keep everyone on track. Displaying your mission statement in prominent areas such as meeting rooms, job trailers and offices can help keep your mission in the minds of your team members.

The idea is to make checking on the partnership a habit

Keep a list of things to improve, you're likely to forget items if you don't

Meet with your other partnering champion(s)

Each partnering champion watches out for what is going well and what needs correction, and keeps the project on track toward accomplishing the mission. The champions can share their different perspectives on a regular basis, and discuss potential actions that might be taken. Personality conflicts, in particular, can be successfully resolved if caught early on. The partnering champion should be constantly on the watch for such conflicts as they can destroy the partnership.

Ask others what they think

It is always a good idea to ask people what they think, how they feel things are going, and what they think needs to be improved to have a successful partnership. The champions should keep track of the answers to these questions. The responses can be invaluable in making any needed adjustments. It is important that the identity of anyone who tells you something is kept confidential, unless they specifically tell you it is not necessary.

Bring information and ideas to meetings

Armed with all the information and ideas for how to continue to improve the partnership, the partnering champions typically lead the evaluation meetings. The champions may from time-to-time want to specifically add items to the evaluation agenda. The champions are there to share what they see, and should be able to call special meetings as necessary to keep the partnering team on track.

The champions are there to share what they see — and should be able to call special meetings as necessary

36

Recommitting

Coming together is a beginning; keeping together is progress, working together is success.

Henry Ford

At the conclusion of your partnering session, commitment and excitement for the project and partnership will be high. Over time, the commitment can naturally wane, especially on longer projects. Recommitting to the partnership and adjusting goals to address changes that were unforeseen at the time you developed your goals is a way to keep the partnership on track, or, if necessary, to get it back on track.

The best method I've seen for recommitment is holding a follow-up partnering session with all of the project partners. Re-partnering can be effective when there are significant personnel changes on the project, or when disputes go unresolved, breaking down trust.

Benefits of Follow-Up Partnering Workshops

Effective for dealing with change
Most kickoff partnering workshops are held just before construction begins. Many significant changes will occur during the project; these changes will alter the challenges the team faces. In a follow-up session you can set your gyroscope once again toward your mission and define the new critical path to its accomplishment.

Useful for dealing with relationship issues
One attorney friend told me of a study conducted by a state bar association on the root causes of construction disputes which end up in litigation. He explained that the study

> *The best method I have seen for recommitment is holding a follow-up partnering session*

showed around 90 percent of construction litigation cases had little or nothing to do with the technical aspects of the job - but rather had to do with relationship issues. Many times something happens between two or more of the project partners that, left unchecked, begins a negative spiral. A follow-up partnering session can help stop the negative spiral, resolve the conflict, and give a fresh start to the relationships.

No one can stay committed to project goals that become unachievable due to circumstances beyond their control

Reassess project goals

As the project proceeds, checking to see if your goals still define your original consensus on what would be a successful project. No one can be committed to goals that have become unachievable because changes have occurred. Adjusting the goals to be achievable under the new project conditions and confirming that everyone is committed to working toward their accomplishment is what your follow-up session(s) accomplish.

Tool for solving conflict

Besides personality issues, other conflicts can arise. Most often I have seen conflicts over roles and responsibilities which lead to misunderstanding who is to do what. Other conflicts can arise over sharing risks and rewards. At the follow-up session these issues can be identified and discussed, and solutions found.

A follow-up partnering session can be a time to celebrate what has been accomplished

Celebration of successes

A follow-up session can be a time for the project team members to step back and see what they have accomplished together. It is usually much more than anyone realizes. This makes people feel appreciated for the effort they've made, and creates a point of ending and a new beginning. It is difficult for team members to stay committed for years. Periodically celebrating what you have accomplished to date helps to give you new energy for the rest of the project.

Deciding to Hold Follow-Up Sessions

Most follow-up sessions are one day in duration, but depending what the objectives are, you may decide to hold a session that could range from half-a-day to a full two days.

Your follow-up session should be custom-designed by your facilitator to meet your desired outcomes. One public agency's experience has been that a third of their projects would probably benefit from a re-partnering workshop. There seem to be two viewpoints in making the decision to follow-up.

When there is a problem
Waiting until there is a problem which needs to be addressed is one way to approach following up. This is practical in that it does not waste time in a meeting where there are no new issues to tackle. One side-effect of meeting only if there is a problem is that everyone on the team feels a tinge of failure because they have to meet again to re-partner.

One practical method is waiting until there is a problem requiring solution

On a regular basis
The other viewpoint is that deciding up-front when follow-up sessions will occur helps to assure a level of commitment. Some teams select a milestone, project phase, or time sequence (e.g. every six months) to automatically hold their follow-up session(s). There is flexibility in this approach; if the team feels, at any given point, they are doing so well that they don't need to hold the follow-up session, they can simply decide not to hold that session.

Potential Follow-Up Agenda

Your agenda will be designed to meet specific objectives for each session. Here is a sample of what might be included in your session agenda.

You need a specific agenda for your follow-up session

Project Memories
Having each team member share his most exciting project memory, along with the names of those who have helped him the most, helps you gain a better perspective of the project from a personal vantage point. This is an excellent way to start the follow-up session.

Lessons Learned
Looking at what is helping and what is hindering success will reveal areas on which you can build further success, and identify areas requiring change.

Revisiting Our Mission and Goals

Evaluating the mission statement to see if it still is what the team sees as its ideal project will ensure that you once again have an agreed-upon target for which to aim.

Evaluating Progress

Evaluating the goals and actions that were developed at the last session to see if they have been completed, are still appropriate, or still are to be attempted, is important. It forces you to remember to what you committed and to honestly look at the effort that has been made.

> *Your follow-up partnering session will end with each team member signing the partnering agreement, once again making their personal commitment*

Key Issues

Some experienced owners and contractors tell me the most important part of repartnering is identifying those key issues which stand in the way of accomplishing your mission, or are absolutely necessary to accomplishing it. This identification creates your new critical path to success. The issues may include those previously identified and/or new ones.

Creative Problem Solving

Going through a creative problem solving process that leads you to agreed-upon goals and actions will put into motion the tasks that will accomplish your new, revised mission.

Recommitting by Signing a Re-Partnering Agreement

Your follow-up sessions will end with each team member signing the partnering agreement, once again making a personal commitment to the accomplishment of the team's mission and goals.

37

Celebrating Successes

People want to feel what they do makes a difference.

Frances Hesselbein
President, The Drucker Foundation

I've already referred several times to the importance of celebrating your successes. It is important enough to say it one more time. Let's look at when, why and what to do to celebrate.

When to Celebrate

Along the way

Making celebration a part of your project requires some forethought and planning. The rewards will be great. Celebrating along the way, as the project progresses, will keep the esprit de corps high and problems minimized. Recognizing and appreciating what is going right is a powerful way to reinforce the partnering spirit on your project. Looking for and finding ways to celebrate will help you and your partnering team experience your project as exciting and rewarding.

> *You can celebrate along the way, save it for the end, or even better, celebrate when it's least expected*

At the end

Many times when a project ends everyone is working to finish the final little pieces, but there is no last day to the project. It just trickles away. Soon everyone is working on their next project. As people move off the project the "end" is anticipated, but never actually celebrated. This can lead to burnout of project team members, and it means that you never meet to learn the final lessons of the project, share the war stories and brag about the challenges you overcame together. Such review and evaluation is essential. Giving the team an emotional ending and celebration can have a dramatic impact on everyone. You worked long and hard to build this project. Some things went as you hoped, others did not, but you worked together, and you did it. Now the project stands as a monument to your effort. This is definitely a time to celebrate!

The key is to listen and do the unexpected

When it is least expected
The element of surprise is powerful. You can use it to create impromptu rewards for people you want to thank and whose efforts you appreciate. Small things can mean a lot. For example, bringing lunch for the crew. Listen to what people tell you they like, then find a way to support their interest. The key is to listen and do the unexpected.

Why to Celebrate

There are many reasons to celebrate, some of which we have already discussed in this book. Below are still more reasons why you should make celebration a part of your project life.

You celebrate to build relationships, lesson tension and enjoy your project, to create an open atmosphere, but most importantly, to say thank you

Build relationships
Celebrating your successes allows for relationships and friendships to develop. Having a good relationship changes most of the project's problems into challenges. Many people who have been in the industry for years tell me that projects just aren't fun anymore, that it's fighting all the way. Working together to accomplish a common goal can bind people together in a special way. You can help by celebrating.

Lessen tension and enjoy your project
As people become tired, particularly if there are countless changes and challenges, tension and stress grow, and tempers shorten. Stopping to say to one another, "Look at what we have done so far," can help to calm things down and keep the project in perspective. Many people who have been in the industry for years say there is no fun left in it. They

see too much confrontation, too much stress, and not enough project team spirit. I have never seen a project that was truly successful if the project team wasn't having a good time at least every now and then. You can help create that good time and help the project team keep its perspective.

Create an atmosphere for creativity and open communication
Celebrating helps to create an atmosphere which allows for open, honest communication. This leads to the team's ability to create solutions together that are mutually beneficial. If people work to get only what they want and don't care if others get what they need, trust will go down the drain rapidly. By appreciating each other's efforts and by celebrating your successes you will be maintaining the atmosphere necessary for partnering to flourish.

> *Only your imagination limits what you can do to celebrate*

To say thank you
Two powerful words — thank you. Not said often enough. It can be in the form of words or actions. A thank you lunch. A thank you hat. A thank you break. It doesn't matter what form your appreciation takes, only that you take time to give it.

What to Do to Celebrate

Photo or Poster
I once walked onto a job site and saw a giant poster of the partnering team hanging on the outside of the job trailer. It was there to show appreciation of their team effort. A photo or poster helps everyone to see that you are a team, you've made commitments to each other, and you are following through — together.

> *There is nothing like having your project team members see their names and pictures in the local newspaper for a job well done*

Press release to local paper
There is nothing like having your project team members see their names and/or pictures in their local paper. A quick press release highlighting the great job they are doing at meeting the challenges of the project brightens everyone's day. You can create good press and good will, and best of all, many organizations already have the contacts necessary to easily make it happen.

Newsletter article

On most projects, one or more of the organizations has an in-house newsletter of magazine. An article highlighting the efforts of specific team members, along with photos, helps to show appreciation to the team and gives others ideas of what might be possible.

Rewards

People will do over and over what is rewarded. Rewards don't have to be big, or costly, they just have to be sincere. A special hat, T-shirt, jacket, coffee mug or special script (partnering bucks) are effective in rewarding those who

Figure 35

make an outstanding partnering effort. Wearing the hat or using the coffee mug shows others that you have been acknowledged for your work.

Special event

A special event can be a barbecue, attending a ball game, playing softball, going bowling, or anything you can imagine that brings the team together to play and have fun, appreciating successes.

Singing telegram

Doing something that is usually only done at parties is a good way to create an atmosphere of celebration. At times I have sent a singing telegram to the team. On the next page is a song that was developed by one project that had been plagued by floods in addition to more routine challenges. The job was to build a fish screen, but many felt it was time to scream. So the title became the fish scream project song.

"Fish Scream" Project Song
Sung to the tune of "The Gambler"

It was 20 years ago a mandate came from the boss
They said something's going to change 'cuz them fish is getting hurt
Three fishes got sucked up in a hydro electric pump
Project "Fish Scream" was born - It was a pain in the rump

A great team came together and boy they had to weather
The controversy, the solid rock through which they had to blast
The project costs 5 million bucks per fish that's lost
It's enough to make the taxpayers just a little cross

> *You got to know how to screen them, and know when to clean 'em*
> *Know when to let 'em flow just knowing what to do*
> *It wasn't easy, kinda made some people queasy*
> *Congratulations for a job well done to a real terrific crew*

Project "Fish Scream" when it started was not for the faint-hearted
There were lots of major obstacles a'floating in the way
We blasted out a tunnel and woke up all the neighbors
All we could say was "Sorry, this isn't child's play"

The project finally finished - way ahead of schedule
Under budget, morale intact and it's environmentally sound
A test of God, the rains came and the river flooded over
Then cheers were heard from the Fish Scream team,
The Project held its ground

> *You got to know how to screen them, and know when to clean 'em*
> *Know when to let 'em flow just knowing what to do*
> *It wasn't easy, kinda made some people queasy*
> *Congratulations for a job well done to a real terrific crew*

Figure 36

PART 4

Special Applications of Partnering

38

Partnering Smaller Projects

Small is Beautiful

Ernst Friedrich Schumacher

What is a Smaller Project?

Smaller is a relative term. What is a small project for one organization is a large project for another. And, if a project is large to even one of your potential partners, it should be regarded as a good candidate for partnering. There is increased risk whenever someone takes on a project that is larger than those to which they are accustomed. For our purposes "smaller" is defined as those projects that are under $3 million.

Several public owners have partnered projects as small as $40,000. The smallest project I have partnered was $400,000. For you what constitutes "smaller" should be determined by your organization and what it is accustomed to doing.

Small and mid-sized projects can benefit from the same partnering principles of large projects

The Benefits of Partnering Smaller Projects

Small and mid-sized projects can benefit from the same partnering principles that large projects have, and for the same reasons. Small projects have many of the same complicating factors. A $3 million project has an architect, an owner, engineers, a client user, contractors, project managers, inspectors, etc., just like a $50 million project. Developing good working relationships as you begin to work together can reduce the risk of unresolved disputes; the inability to deal effectively with unforeseen conditions; and defensive positioning.

With a shorter duration everything becomes more urgent. You have less time to develop your team, open honest communications, develop trust, or co-create solutions. You have less time to get everything right.

Because many smaller projects are, by definition, of a shorter duration, it becomes critical that decisions be made and resolutions found rapidly. There often simply isn't time for an error, or else the project is delayed or is over budget.

A one week delay might be tolerable on a large project — and disastrous on a small one

Potential Benefits

- Reduced risk of claims and litigation
- Improved working relationships
- Reduced paperwork
- Improved job-site safety
- Win/win solutions to problems
- Increased flexibility
- Helps contain costs
- Completed on or ahead of schedule
- Problems are resolved quickly
- Quality is maintained

Partnering Smaller Projects is Just as Important as Partnering Large Projects

I have conducted sessions as brief as four hours with excellent results

Size is just one factor in your project. Some small projects are extremely complex, political, important or sensitive, or have a strict, mandated schedule. These circumstances can make partnering the smaller project more significant than partnering a larger one.

Often there is less room for error with smaller projects, given their tight schedules. Unforeseen conditions, such as unknown utilities, can destroy the schedule. Creativity is required to adjust staging and activities to keep the project moving. If the project team is not working together, the project can end in disaster. Developing a means for open communications and having processes in place for problem solving can be the difference between success and failure.

The Smaller Project Workshop

For most smaller projects a one-day workshop is recommended. However, four-hour, or even three-hour, workshops can produce excellent results. A skilled facilitator will know how to guide your workshop to focus on relationship-building, problem-solving or other project challenges. Several of my clients set aside a morning or afternoon, or select an evening workshop. The results of this shorter version work best if the partnering team is already familiar with the partnering process and principles.

Sample Half-Day Session Outline (4 hours)

> Introductions/Interests
> Partnering Overview
> Mission
> Key Project Issues
> Creative Problem Solving
> Goals/Actions
> Dispute Resolution
> Evaluation
> Signing the Partnering Agreement

A whole day spent on partnering and the pre-job conference for some small projects seems like overkill. For them a two or three-hour session blended, with the pre-job conference, has worked well, but is not optimal.

Sample Partnering/Pre-Job Workshop Outline (2.5/1.5 hrs - 4 hours total)

> Introductions
> Partnering Overview
> Weak Links
> Evaluation/Commitment
> Dispute Resolution
> Evaluating Progress
> Signing the Partnering Agreement

Combining the partnering session with the pre-job conference is an efficient use of time

"I would recommend you consider a full day session from a cost/benefit standpoint. I believe that even a $500k project can afford an extra $2-4k expense initially for the payback in both hard and soft dollars that a successfully partnered project brings."
Dennis Dunne
Director, GSA
Santa Clara County

The more people there are, the more time it takes to give each participant a chance to share their perspectives and ideas. Therefore these short workshops should be limited to seven to fifteen people. You will not accomplish much with a larger group.

Avoid the temptation to facilitate your own session

Spending more time together does help relationships evolve. Sometimes what seems to be an inordinate amount of time spent on partnering turns out to be time well spent should you run into some critical problems on the project.

To Facilitate or not to Facilitate

To successfully execute a short partnering session and get through all of the vital components that will make your partnership work takes skill and experience. It is highly recommend that you use a professional facilitator. Some clients have shared their horror stories with me of attempts to facilitate their own partnering sessions. Most often there is such a power imbalance between the "leader" who is facilitating and the project partners that barriers often get built higher. The presence of a neutral, professional facilitator, who has spent time to understand the project and the players, and has designed a process to get you to where you need to be in the time allotted, is your best insurance for a successful partnership.

39

Advanced Project Partnering

To boldly go where no man has gone before

Gene Rodenberry

Partnering has proven itself as a means for improving the quality of the construction process (see Part 1). The vast majority of partnering occurs at the beginning of the project's construction phase. Many people are expanding their use of partnering, and discovering new methods for utilizing the partnering process to help their project. Here are a few of the different methods now being used.

Many people are discovering new uses for the partnering process to help their project

Turn-Around Partnering

When a dispute erupts on a project it often harms the working relationships. A turn-around partnering session can help resolve the dispute, begin to heal the relationships and get the project back on track. If a dispute occurs during construction, especially in the early phases of a project, it can significantly jeopardize the completion of the project, which is probably still a long way in the future. Project stakeholders may begin to push responsibilities (and blame) onto others. But the project still must be built, and now there is a war going on.

Turn-around partnering is a process for resolving a project dispute and healing relationships

Turn-around partnering can work whether your project was originally partnered or not. Sometimes the dispute has already been resolved, but relationships have been damaged. Sometimes the dispute can be resolved during the partnering workshop, and other times an agreed-upon process can be developed during the session for resolving the dispute. Turn-around partnering helps to set the stage for the project's completion without hostility.

It can be almost unbearable to work on a project that can't escape the conflict and animosity that continuously grows from an unresolved dispute. The partnering process brings everyone back to the table to talk, work out differences and find solutions. The project has to be completed one way or another; it can be either in a war zone, or, by declaring a cease-fire and working out a treaty, peacefully. A turn-around partnering session serves as the peace talks.

I have seen the partnering process bring everyone back to the table to talk and work out their differences

Program Partnering

Program partnering is a series of partnering sessions designed to address the separate stages of a project, or a series of smaller related projects. By developing a partnering program, the scope and sequence of the partnering effort is aligned to the particular project for greater overall results. Program partnering works well on multiple-prime projects. With five, seven, twenty or more prime contractors working on a project it is impractical to bring them all together at a kickoff session. By conducting a partnering session at each phase of the project, those prime contractors who are a part of that phase come together to discuss coordination, communication, and project issues, and develop a mission, goals, action plans and dispute and evaluation processes.

Program partnering is a series of partnering sessions designed to address the separate stages of a project

Program partnerings can also be designed for a series of projects. Often the first session is conducted to set the parameters for the entire program, under which each project will be directed. This first session acts like an umbrella, with each subsequent partnering and project falling under the objectives of the program partnering's umbrella.

The program approach to multiple prime projects has been very successful. It also has worked on some large, complex projects, where we divided the partnering into phases so that commitment and coordination could be revisited at each phase of the project.

This approach also works well for design/build projects. You can design a partnering process to help everyone work together to design and build the best project possible.

A typical sequence for a program partnering for a single large, complex project might be:

- Strategic or kickoff session
- Site partnering, including all the site contractors
- Shell partnering, including all the building shell contractors
- Interior partnering, including all building systems construction
- Finishing partnering, including all the finishing trades
- Turn-over/activation partnering, including all the vendors and operations people

Partnering can help two public agencies involved in the same project to work together

Of course, the number of workshops will vary according to your specific project's needs. Each workshop leads to the next, building on each other. Each is based on the same partnering principles, creates an overall project culture, builds confidence in the participants and commitment to the common goals everyone shares.

Inter-Agency Partnering

When two public agencies have a project in common an inter-agency partnering can be useful and have dramatic results. This is especially true if the agencies need to work together to be successful. An inter-agency partnering might include a city, county, municipality, or a local, state, or federal agency.

A key result is identifying and agreeing to the roles and responsibilities of each agency

Inter-agency partnering allows for multiple agencies to build a common vision and mission for the project. There may be more than two, but for this discussion I will assume there are only two. Some projects have more than one public owner, and some projects have several agencies with which they must interface, gain approvals, or negotiate agreements even if the agencies are at odds with each other. Inter-agency partnering helps break down old, traditional barriers and build a new more productive relationship. Identifying and agreeing on the roles and responsibilities of each agency as they relate to the project, along with co-creating methods and means for working together, goes a long way toward eliminating the adversarial approach so many agencies have with one another.

These multiple agency partnerings have had tremendous success. In one instance twenty different agencies successfully partnered together to develop an environmental plan; in another, seven agencies came together to minimize the impact of a major airport expansion. These involved projects where conflict had been present for many years, and litigation had been the method for resolving differences. The inter-agency partnering provided a forum for cooperation, understanding and problem-solving.

Environmental Partnering

An environmental partnering takes place during the planning phase of the project. Many times environmental documents are not forthcoming because agreement on what they need to contain, or on whose information is correct, cannot be reached. I have seen projects stalled for three to four years in this phase. An environmental partnering brings everyone together to decide on what is required, what are potential changes and the impacts of those changes, and whose data to use (or to jointly collect data) so there is agreement. All the key regulatory agencies are brought together to understand and agree on a process for completing this critical phase of the project.

One recent project had been stalled for three years. After a one-day workshop an agreement was reached as to what would be needed to go forward. Specific dates were agreed to and, after years of frustration, the project went forward. Bringing everyone into the same room at the same time to listen to what each party needed shortened the process by months, if not years.

Incentives Partnering

Some owners have the ability to write incentives into their contracts; should a contractor or designer complete the

> *All of the key regulatory agencies are brought together to understand and agree on a process for completing this phase of the project*

> *The parties come together to define by what criteria success will be measured*

project within some predefined parameters an incentive is paid them. An incentive partnering session is one where the designer, contractor, and owner come together to define by what criteria success will be measured, and incentives paid accordingly.

An incentive partnering has many of the components of a project partnering session, but goes into more detail as to what the participants see as their critical path to success. Incentive partnerings for design/build projects are exciting and can have dramatic and excellent results. Projects with incentive language help create an atmosphere conducive to partnering because everyone has worked together to create the criteria by which success will be measured. It really is something to see.

Often the intent of the design is lost in the details, leading to confusion when changes must be made

Design Intent Partnering

Design teams generally do a great job in providing the details of the design, however, many times the intent of the design is not well communicated to the contractor and subs, or well understood by the owner or construction manager. Many projects have more than one designer. An entire team of architects and/or engineers works to create the design. Some projects use as many as twenty or more design firms. Understanding and agreeing on the design intent for each of the design packages can go a long way in assisting the owner, contractor, construction manager, and designers in making good decisions as the project rolls out.

Identifying the key areas of design and their overriding intent sets the parameters for creating solutions to the problems that will arise during construction. Many times a design team develops its portion of the design, working alone, and it is then incorporated into the overall job package. It has been my experience that the individual design teams often doesn't see the whole picture of the project. Sometimes the intent of the project gets lost in the process, especially in the confusion of trying to meet schedules or solve problems.

Conflicts over ownership can play havoc on a project

Design intent partnering is an opportunity to focus in on the design intent, gain an understanding of that intent, identify possible problem areas, define roles and responsibilities, and to resolve design problems.

Multiple Owner Partnering

Some projects have more than one owner. The project may have one owner at design and construction, another upon completion, and yet another within the operations organization. Conflicts over ownership can play havoc on a project. This problem is prevalent when one organization is providing funding, another will take overall ownership upon the project's completion, while still others will take individual ownership as they move into their section of the completed project. On one project I am facilitating there are seven different "owners"; the city, the county, the owner's agent, the operations/systems people, the display people, the vendors, and a nonprofit foundation which will oversee and collect funds from visitors.

A power struggle can result between multiple owners

With multiple owners, each having their own interests, a power struggle can result on the project. Decision making becomes slow and difficult. Multiple-owner partnering clarifies the roles and responsibilities of each owner, defines a decision-making process, and clarifies areas of influence or the point in time when ownership shifts. These definitions, roles and responsibilities, and processes need to be communicated with the contractors.

Community Partnering

Communities today have a greater say than ever in whether a project goes forward — community partnering brings the community onto the project team

Each of our projects is built within a community. People within the community frequently have strong feelings about the project, and can dramatically impact the project, or stop it all together. A community partnering brings together all of the project participants, along with community representatives. Together they work to understand their different interests and what the community needs. They then work together to find ways to give everyone what they need (mutual gain).

Often so little true communication goes on between the community and the project stakeholders that neither side has

220

ever really "heard" the other before. Now with understanding and a commitment to try to cooperate, they can create solutions that no one had ever considered before.

Some ways this process can work is helping to:

- Negotiate a freeway agreement
- Agree on an affirmative action process
- Negotiate a use agreement
- Negotiate right-of-way agreements

Value Engineering Workshop

Most design teams and many construction mangers perform various value engineering tasks. Often this is done individually by the person charged with viewing the project from a value engineering perspective, rather than by the entire project team.

A value engineering workshop held with all of the designers, the contractor, key subcontractors and the owner can dramatically improve the value engineering process, while maintaining the integrity of the design.

Most effective workshops happen when there is a clear dollar amount by which we are seeking to reduce the total project cost, and when there is a clear understanding of the most important aspects of the design. This understanding serves to maintain design quality and intent while allowing for creativity in reducing the overall cost of the project.

My most effective value engineering workshops occur when there is a specific dollar amount by which we must reduce costs

Constructability Workshop

A constructability workshop brings together the design team, owner, and contractor representatives for the sole purpose of discussing the best means and methods for constructing a project.

The most beautiful design is pointless if it cannot be built

As more owners move to design/build as their project delivery system, holding a constructability review when the project is still in its conceptual stage can drastically improve the project's chances for success, and reduce overall cost.

For private projects, the contractor may already be known, or a small list of qualified contractors may exist. For low-bid projects, it is difficult to bring in contractors and not taint the bidding process. In this case retired contractors or special consultants may be secured.

The constructability workshop gives the design team and owner a construction perspective at the point in the project when it can do the most good — before the project is fully designed, or at least before it is put out for bid.

40

Special Application Partnering

Only those societies with a high degree of social trust will be able to create the kind of flexible, large-scale business organizations that are needed for successful competition in the emerging global economy.
Francis Fukuuyama

Partnering is not just for the construction phase of projects, but has several variations which work well in other areas. This chapter presents a few of the applications I have been involved with recently. New applications are evolving all the time. Partnering is a tool which can be used to accomplish many different things. It is limited only by your imagination. As a piano is an instrument for music, partnering is a tool for problem-solving and cooperation. On a piano you might choose to play Bach, boogie-woogie, or jazz. So, too, with the partnering tool; you can apply it in many different situations.

General Contractor and Subcontractors

Forging a partnership between a general contractor and key subcontractors helps everyone. This can be with all the subcontractors on a specific project, or for a select few key subcontractors you will be doing business with over and over again. Most often it is with the general and their key subcontractors. Together they create shared administrative processes, build trust, strengthen lines of communication, and may even sponsor management training and other skill-building. The objective is to help everyone be more successful. By working as a team, each business can be more productive; there isn't the fear that the contractor will harm the subs in order to save his profits.

Partnering is a tool which is limited only by your imagination

While the general contractor usually initiates this process, inviting the subcontractors to participate, it also is important that the subs pay for some portion of the process. This helps to gain their buy-in and lessens the power imbalance between the general and subs. This form of partnering has worked remarkably well with forward-thinking general contractors who are seeking to improve their overall project quality. The risk is high for both the general and the subcontractors on projects. Working together to forge a partnership before the project is bid, without a specific project in mind, or when subs are being named, can go a long way in reducing the risk for everyone.

An internal partnering works to break down the barriers within an organization

Internal Partnering

Often within organizations turf protecting, conflicts, and even cultural differences make it difficult for separate units to work together. Internal partnering works to break down barriers and gets the organizational units working together.

There are some natural schisms within organizations: estimating and the field crews, design and construction, management and labor, or accounting and operations. The internal partnering process brings everyone together to create a strategy for working together more effectively.

Sometimes an internal conflict within one organization can bring the entire project to a halt

It is not unusual for internal conflicts to have a dramatic impact on projects. I have been in several partnering sessions where the people within one organization had more conflict and disagreements than the entire partnering team combined. In such sessions the path for mutual gain was to spend a good portion of our time helping them solve some of their internal conflicts so the project could go forward.

Internal partnering is a beginning for breaking down internal barriers, but a onetime effort is not sufficient to keep the gaps from growing back. Some method of bringing key leaders together on an continuing basis to evaluate and adjust the goals set by the partnering team must be implemented. Above all it takes commitment.

Lessons Learned Partnering

Capturing the lessons from your projects and communicating them to everyone in your organization, so that the lessons are learned, is a challenge. Far too often we move on to the next project, and then the next, without understanding the lessons that should have been learned along the way, missing an opportunity to increase our organization's knowledge base. Shortening your organization's learning curve can give you a step up on your competition and improve the quality of your projects.

Those who forget the past are doomed to repeat it

This partnering session is about a specific project's lessons, and usually is limited to one company or organization. However, lessons learned partnerings can be conducted with the entire partnering team. The objective is to close out the project by exploring what lessons were learned, or can be learned. What went right, and what did you learn from it; what went wrong, and what did you learn? How will you incorporate these experiences into future projects? You will capture the most important lessons learned, see how new processes were created, or how old processes didn't work.

The most important aspect of the lessons learned partnering session is that after you capture the lessons learned you record them and communicate them to your entire organization.

Even if there isn't a specific project involved, partnering can help two organizations work better together

Inter-Agency/Organizational Partnering

Inter-agency/organizational partnering can assist two agencies or organizations that need to work together more effectively, even though there is not a specific project involved. This might occur when one agency is at the service of another. Or, it might be when an agency and a private organization are working together to achieve a specific goal. Whenever you bring two or more separate organizations together the chances for conflict are great. Inter-agency/organizational partnering works to break down organizational barriers and develops a shadow organization (see Chapter 10) which can achieve the partnership's objectives.

Labor and Management Partnering

Prior to negotiating a new labor agreement, or when there is rising conflict and a labor action is possible, a labor and management partnering can help bring things into a more cooperative state. Labor and management have mutual interests as do project stakeholders. As on a project, only with great difficulty can either choose to leave the relationship. So it is best if they work together to make things better for both.

Holding a partnering session just prior to the onset of contract negotiations can help both sides negotiate better agreements

Holding a partnering session just prior to the onset of contract negotiations can help both sides negotiate better agreements. Once positioning stops and listening starts, the team can begin to create ways to improve its lot.

Developing skills together, such as negotiating and effective listening, gives everyone common language and actions to use in improving their communication. This approach stopped a Teamster's strike in California which was imminent. Both sides agreed to postpone the strike for one year and try partnering. Within a few months a new agreement was struck, and the relationship shifted from adversarial to cooperative. It really does work.

Strategic Partnering

Strategic partnering entails one or more organizations coming together for a strategic reason. In a strategic partnering an alliance is created because each organization has something to offer the other that will increase its value. So the organizations are more valuable together than apart.

A strategic partnering forms an alliance between two or more organizations for mutual gain

The strategic partnering process explores the strengths of each organization and the needs of the marketplace, and then creates a strategy for combining the organizations' strengths to create a competitive advantage in the market.

Strategic partnering also must address how the organizations will work together. You have two distinctly different organizations. By co-creating a mission, goals, and methods the organizations can avoid suffering from clashes and can focus on working together to accomplish their goals.

Strategic reasons for partnering might include:

- Gaining a cost advantage through
- Economics of scale
- Learning
- Forward/backward integration
- Location

Gaining a scope advantage through
- Product/service line
- Vertical integration
- Geography
- Transferring skills
- Shared activities

Strategic reasons for partnering might include gaining either a cost advantage or scope advantage

41

ADR Techniques in Building and Construction

Never, never, never, never give up.

Winston Churchill

Alternative dispute resolution (ADR) is a growing wave within the design, building, and construction industry. Frustrated with litigation and its overwhelming time and expense, owners, contractors, and designers are looking for new ways to resolve project disputes. At a construction conference I attended, one of the lawyers stood up and boldly stated that partnering and ADR were so effective in preventing and resolving project disputes, that construction lawyers are having to redefine their role, and that within five years there may not be a need for construction litigation.

Well, I'm not sure about the elimination of litigation, but certainly partnering and other forms of dispute resolution are changing the nature of construction. One reason for this change is that the majority of construction disputes which end up in litigation are not technical in nature, but have to do with relationship issues. Ego, hurt feelings, resentment, frustration — all of these lead people to court.

Partnering and other forms of dispute prevention and resolution are changing the nature of construction

Hierarchy of Alternative Dispute Resolution Processes

There is a hierarchy to ADR, with each succeeding process becoming more formalized, and control shifting from the parties controlling agreements to a third party deciding. All of the processes on the left side of the following figure are controlled by the parties involved in the dispute. All of those on the right side are controlled by someone else.

ADR is much less costly and faster than litigation. Costs escalate with litigation due to the discovery process — the more discovery the higher the tab. Since there is little or no discovery with most forms of ADR, your costs will be dramatically lower. You may also find that your agreements are more lasting.

Partnering is the first level of ADR, it works to prevent disputes from occurring

Hierarchy of Alternative Dispute Resolution Processes

Parties Control Agreement	Third Party Decides for Parties
Partnering	Dispute Review Boards
Negotiation	Arbitration
Facilitated Negotiation	Mini-trial
On-site Neutral	Settlement Conference
Mediation	Litigation

Figure 37

Negotiating is the second stage of ADR — the parties try to resolve the dispute themselves

Processes Where the Parties Control the Outcome

Partnering
Partnering is the first level in the ADR hierarchy. It works to prevent disputes. This entire book, up to this point, has been about how to make partnering work for your projects. It is, and will continue to be, the first line of defense against project claims, disputes and litigation.

Negotiation
When there is a problem, negotiation between the concerned parties is what you do to try to solve the problem. Most

conflicts will be solved through negotiation. This entails collecting information about the problem and then meeting and coming to agreement on how to proceed. The better you can become at win/win negotiating, the less risk you have of conflicts escalating. Note: few construction managers, owners, or project managers know how to negotiate non-adversarially — instead, they quickly move to positions and become adversarial. I highly recommend training in this area.

Facilitated Negotiation

If your attempt at negotiating an agreement was unsuccessful, a facilitated negotiation might work. Here a neutral, skilled negotiator is brought in to help the parties negotiate an agreement. This is an informal process. The presence of a neutral usually allows for an agreement to be struck.

Mediation brings in a third party who is neutral to help the parties come to agreement

On-site Neutral

Some projects choose to have an on-site neutral. The on-site neutral can be used in two ways. One is to select the on-site neutral and have her act as the neutral for all issues for the entire project. More frequently, a second method is being used, particularly for technical issues. An on-site neutral, usually with specialized knowledge or experience related to the issue at hand, is selected at the time the dispute arises and comes in to assist in the resolution of the technical issue involved. Thus, there may be more than one on-site neutral over the life of the project. Either way, the on-site neutral helps the parties understand and agree on a solution to the dispute.

A trained mediator does not force an agreement upon the parties

Mediation

Mediation is rapidly growing as a preferred method of dispute resolution. Here a trained mediator helps the parties come to resolution. A trained mediator utilizes many techniques to move the parties closer together, achieving a durable agreement.

There is no one way to mediate. A mediator's style is often a result of his/her background. Many people from different professions have entered the field of mediation. On one hand you have litigators, who after twenty years of litigating disputes, feel that they want to try their hand at mediation. Some former litigators (and former judges) see mediation as an opportunity to be lawyer, judge and jury, and work to beat-up and wear-down the parties until they submit. This is the Attila the Hun approach to mediation. Far too often the agreements fall apart when the "mediator" leaves.

The other end of the spectrum attracted to mediation are family counselors and therapists. Their approach is to investigate "how it feels" rather than to explore options and solutions to the problems at hand. The message here is to select a mediator who has the right approach for your dispute, and has a track record of helping parties create durable agreements. Ask your facilitator for help in selecting a suitable mediator.

Dispute review boards have become prevalent in the construction industry

Processes Where a Third-Party Decides

Dispute Review Board
Dispute review boards are selected at the beginning of construction. They usually consist of three people. One is selected by the contractor and one by the owner. These two then select the third member. Each side of the dispute makes its case to the board, then the board makes a decision. The decision can be binding or nonbinding depending upon the contract or agreement between the parties.

On multiple prime projects the dispute review board is replaced by a board of adjustments

Dispute review board language has become prevalent in construction specifications, and it works. It works because nobody wants to go before the dispute review board, so they come to agreement just before the board is to convene.

Board of Adjustments
Dispute review boards are difficult to maintain on multiple prime projects since you might have to have as many as twenty different boards. A board of adjustments offers a different approach. A board of adjustments is comprised of two parties selected by the owner from the owner's team (and who are not a part of the particular dispute), and two selected by the prime contractor from the contractor's team (who, again, are not a part of the dispute).

Each side states its case before the four board members, with the board members asking questions. Then the parties to the dispute leave and the board caucuses and makes a finding. While this process can be binding, it usually is not.

Arbitration

Arbitration takes many different forms, just as mediation does. Some organizations' approach to arbitration is formal, following the processes of litigation. You might have one arbitrator or a panel of three. The arbitrator(s) is selected and agreed to by both parties. Often there are expert witnesses, discovery, and all the trappings of court. Opponents of this formal approach say it can take almost as long as litigation and can be just as expensive.

Sometimes arbitration can take as long as a law suit

Another approach to arbitration is to have your dispute heard in front of your peers. This approach selects an experienced arbitrator who is also an expert from your field, and who is acceptable to both sides, to serve as arbitrator. He/she listens to both sides, and then renders a decision. Formal or informal, arbitration can be binding or nonbinding.

Mini-Trial

Simulated court rooms have been built in office buildings in which to hold mini-trials. A retired judge usually presides over the case and renders a decision. I have heard of mock juries being the decision-makers in some disputes. This form of ADR is a private litigation process. It is much faster than going through the judicial process, and it can be binding or nonbinding.

A settlement conference is the last chance to settle before things go to trial

Many times the mini-trial offers everyone a chance to see what would happen if the case were to go to court. With this insight, a settlement can usually be struck.

Settlement Conference

Before you get to trial, the judge will probably require a settlement conference. More and more judges have the ability to select a special master to oversee your settlement, and can even assign an ADR process to your case. A settlement conference and/or a special master is your last chance to come to agreement before you go to trial.

Litigation

You are probably all too familiar with litigation. But I want to make what might be an obvious point, **that litigation is not a good method for resolving most disputes**. It takes too long, costs too much, doesn't create fair decisions and damages relationships. However, on the plus side, litigation is a viable tool for setting precedents. Precedent-setting is responsible for changing many of the methods we use today. It can assist in changing or overturning unfair laws or conditions. However, the outcome from litigation on construction disputes is often lose-lose in terms of time, energy, and money spent. It should not be your first alternative, but your last!

Litigation is not a good method for resolving most disputes

A Multiple Menu Approach to ADR

You do not have to choose just one method of ADR for your project. You can select from the entire menu of ADR processes. The larger and more complex the project, the more methods you might want to have. For example, on a $50 million project you might have:

- Partnering
- Facilitated Negotiation
- Mediation
- Dispute Review Board
- Litigation

You don't have to choose just one method of ADR

You would then have four chances to resolve the dispute before you get to litigation. For a smaller project you might have partnering and a dispute review board or an on-site neutral. The idea is that you have more than one process from which to select, and a predefined order in which to select them. Each one reduces your risk of getting to litigation.

As you can see, you have many options available to your project to keep you out of court and help you resolve project disputes in a fast, cost-effective manner. Use them — they really work!

Epilogue

Peace is not passive, it is active. It stands flexible in the currents of change.

Sue Dyer

Well there you have it - the steps to partnering success. Now it's up to you to take these proven methods and begin immediately to put them into action. Remember, these ideas work. So, if you try something and it doesn't work for you, don't give up. Just tweak it a little until it does work. I leave you with these final thoughts.

Process = Results

Partnering is a process. No matter how many times you have gone through the process with others, it is necessary to go through the process with your current team in order to develop consensus among the team members. However, the time it takes to develop consensus can be significantly shortened when those involved already embody the principles and spirit of partnering.

A Critical Mass

When enough people understand, accept, and implement the principles of partnering, we will have a critical mass. A critical mass is the amount of a given material or the number of people embracing an idea that sustains a chain reaction. If we can gain critical mass, we will have a fundamental shift in the way we do business with each other — we will cooperate instead of being adversaries, seek solutions, not winners. We will find ways to improve our projects rather than spending our resources on finding fault.

The benefit of achieving this critical mass for partnering is that we will then have the atmosphere required to truly innovate and improve productivity. Construction impacts all other industries. Every business must have a place in which to conduct business, transportation to and from their suppliers and customers, and, like every business, construction creates jobs, providing people the means to purchase goods from yet other businesses. If we are to complete in the new global marketplace, we must find ways to improve our productivity and increase innovation.

Leading Edge

Those owners, contractors, designers, and construction managers who learn early-on how to live the principles of partnering on their projects will have a decided advantage. Those who really commit to the partnering principles and apply the partnering spirit on their projects are achieving significant, long-term results. Partnering can truly become a competitive advantage in the marketplace for those who learn how to implement it successfully.

A Universal Idea

Partnering does not just apply to construction. It has applications in almost every other industry, either on projects (i.e. software design or marketing campaigns), or between any grouping of people who must work together for results (i.e. doctors/nurses, labor/management, accounting/operations). The principles are universal; don't limit them only to construction projects.

Go Forth and Partner

Partnering is a tool for project peace. It is not a panacea and will not solve all of your project problems. However, it is the best tool we have available to help manage the risks on projects and improve our results. The women who only owns a hammer sees the solution to every problem as pounding a nail. Partnering offers a new tool box of skills that transcend projects and construction — it can be used in all aspects of our lives — to bring peace and creativity. So, go forth and partner!

References

Chapter 1. Sᴛᴀʏ Oᴜᴛ ᴏғ Cᴏᴜʀᴛ

1. "Lawyers costing economy $500 billion a year," *Contra Costa Times*, 3 April 1991.
2. Walter K. Olson, *The Litigation Explosion: What Happened When America Unleashed the Lawsuit* (New York:Truman Talley Books/Plume Printing, 1992), 10.
3. Olson, *The Litigation Explosion*, 53.
4. Olson, *The Litigation Explosion*, 53.
5. Olson, *The Litigation Explosion*, 299.
6. Olson, *The Litigation Explosion*, 300.
7. Jim Hinze and Bruce Dammeier, "Litigation Proliferation: Survey Finds Causes," *CB&E*, 17 September 1990, 22.

Chapter 2. Dᴏɴ'ᴛ Lᴇᴛ ᴛʜᴇ Pᴀsᴛ Pʀᴇᴅɪᴄᴛ Yᴏᴜʀ Pʀᴏᴊᴇᴄᴛ's Fᴜᴛᴜʀᴇ

8. Sue Dyer, "Partnering: Negotiating the Adversarial Gap," *Proceedings of Inc. Magazine Fifth Annual Conference on Growing the Company* (November 5-6, 1992), 104.

Chapter 4. Mᴀɴᴀɢᴇ Pʀᴏᴊᴇᴄᴛ Rɪsᴋs

9. The Construction Industry Institute Contracting Phase II Task Force, *Cost/Trust Relationship*, Publication 24-1, November 1993, 28.

Chapter 5. Iᴍᴘʀᴏᴠᴇ Pʀᴏᴅᴜᴄᴛɪᴠɪᴛʏ, Qᴜᴀʟɪᴛʏ, ᴀɴᴅ Jᴏʙ Sᴀᴛɪsғᴀᴄᴛɪᴏɴ

10. The Business Roundtable, *Measuring Productivity in Construction,* Report A-1, September, 1982.

Chapter 6. Tʜᴇ Hɪsᴛᴏʀʏ ᴏғ Pᴀʀᴛɴᴇʀɪɴɢ

11. W. Edwards Deming, *Out of Crisis*, (Massachusetts Institute of Technology Center for Advanced Engineering Study, 1986), 23.
12. "85% of DOT's use partnering on projects," *Better Roads*, February 1994, 29.

The International Partnering Institute

Sue Dyer founded the International Partnering Institute as an educational organization dedicated to spreading the partnering concepts worldwide.

The Institute offers training programs which teach the concepts necessary to make partnering a business reality. IPI training courses include:

- The Art of Facilitation
- Professional Facilitator Series
- Advanced Facilitator Practicum
- Non-Adversarial Negotiating
- Building a Partnership between Labor and Management
- Designing an Organizational Dispute Resolution System
- Strategic Marketing for Professionals
- Marketing Planning Intensive
- Developing Your Cooperative Advantage

A brochure with further information about The Institute's training programs is available upon request.

The Institute also offers a certification in Professional Partnering Facilitation. Those receiving certification are ready to successfully market, design and facilitate the partnering process. Applications may be obtained from The Institute; enrollment is limited.

The International Partnering Institute acknowledges individuals who are committed to spreading the partnering concepts by annually awarding the prestigious *Partnering Champion* award.

> *"As the business world becomes a global marketplace, our success hinges on our ability to work together, find strengths in differences, solve problems, and foster cooperation among a number of diverse companies and organizations who can dramatically impact our outcomes. Partnering is the best tool we have to help foster the atmosphere that is needed for business success in the next millennium."*
>
> Sue Dyer

If you would like more information about the International Partnering Institute or its training programs please contact:

International Partnering Institute
1789 Barcelona Street
Livermore, CA 94550
(510)* 455-7850
Fax (510) 443-8318
* The area code will change to 925 in March, 1998

About the Author

Sue Dyer, MBA, was the first woman in the United States to head up a major collective bargaining unit for the construction industry. She is president of **ORG•METRICS**, a consulting firm specializing in dispute resolution and prevention. Sue is founder and president of the Center for Community Dispute Settlement and the International Partnering Institute. Ms. Dyer is known internationally as an accomplished facilitator and mediator, as well as an entertaining and dynamic speaker. She facilitates partnering workshops for over fifty construction projects each year, in addition to mediating disputes and finding new applications for the partnering process and conducting training in facilitation, negotiation and business practices. Her partnering facilitation abilities are renowned, often accomplishing what others said was impossible. With her background in construction, collective bargaining, conflict resolution, negotiation, training design, professional speaking, and mediation, Sue offers an interdisciplinary approach to partnering and mediation, making her services highly regarded and sought after. You can email your questions, ideas, comments and stories to SueDyer@aol.com or contact her at:

1789 Barcelona Street
Livermore, CA 94550
(510)* 449-8300   fax (510) 449-0945
* The area code will change to 925 in March, 1998

Forthcoming Books by Sue Dyer

Howdy Partner

A field manual for project partnering, *Howdy Partner* is written for all of those who work on your construction projects. It takes everyone's commitment for partnering to be successful. Often only project managers and above attend the partnering workshop. This leave many people on the project without the knowledge of partnering or the commitments which have been made among the project team. This books acts as a guide to the partnering concept and fosters commitment from everyone who works on a partnered project. It is also serves as a refresher for those who did attend the partnering workshop to help them stay on track.

Coming in Fall 1997

Built on Trust

Trust is the pinnacle on which all team based performance is based. Working at building trust on projects and within teams is the purpose of *Built On Trust*. The first half of the book discusses the nature of trust, what is it, and is not, along with ways of achieving trust. The second part of the book includes 52 weekly exercises that are designed to help build trust among any group or team.

Coming in Summer 1998

Non-Adversarial Negotiating

Good negotiating skills are the foundation for resolving conflicts, creating solutions to problems, and forming durable agreements. Non-adversarial Negotiating is an approach which seeks to understand others' needs, so solutions and agreements can be created that give each party what they need. Negotiating the best deal possible is not an easy task. It is filled with complications, challenges, frustrations, and opportunities, Incorporating almost twenty years of experience, this book outlines a proven method of negotiating that will help you develop a negotiating strategy, build relationships as you negotiate, and work toward mutually beneficial agreements, often doing what others' say is "impossible".

Coming in Fall 1999

Index